D1221374

The Music
Library

The History of
Punk Rock

Other Books in the Series

The History of American Folk Music
The History of the Blues
The History of Classical Music
The History of Country Music
The History of Gospel Music
The History of Indie Rock
The History of Jazz
The History of Latin Music
The History of Rap and Hip Hop
The History of Reggae
The History of Rock and Roll
The History of World Music
The Instruments of Music

The Music Library

The History of Punk Rock

By Brenden Masar

LUCENT BOOKS

An imprint of Thomson Gale, a part of The Thomson Corporation

Detroit • New York • San Francisco • San Diego • New Haven, Conn. • Waterville, Maine • London • Munich

© 2006 Thomson Gale, a part of The Thomson Corporation.

Thomson and Star Logo are trademarks and Gale and Lucent Books are registered trademarks used herein under license.

For more information, contact
Lucent Books
27500 Drake Rd.
Farmington Hills, MI 48331-3535
Or you can visit our Internet site at http://www.gale.com

LIBRARY OF CONGRESS CATALOGING-IN-PUBLICATION DATA

Masar, Brenden, 1983-
  The history of punk rock / by Brenden Masar.
    p. cm. — (The music library)
  Includes bibliographical references (p.   ) and index.
  ISBN 1-59018-738-5 (hard cover : alk. paper) 1. Punk rock music—History and criticism—Juvenile literature. I. Title. II. Series: Music library (San Diego, Calif.)
  ML3534.M4317 2006
  781.66—dc22

                                                        2005031168

Printed in the United States of America

• Contents •

• Foreword •

In the nineteenth century, English novelist Charles Kingsley wrote, "Music speaks straight to our hearts and spirits, to the very core and root of our souls. . . . Music soothes us, stirs us up . . . melts us to tears." As Kingsley stated, music is much more than just a pleasant arrangement of sounds. It is the resonance of emotion, a joyful noise, a human endeavor that can soothe the spirit or excite the soul. Musicians can also imitate the expressive palate of the earth, from the violent fury of a hurricane to the gentle flow of a babbling brook.

The word *music* is derived from the fabled Greek muses, the children of Apollo who ruled the realms of inspiration and imagination. Composers have long called upon the muses for help and insight. Music is not merely the result of emotions and pleasurable sensations, however.

Music is a discipline subject to formal study and analysis. It involves the juxtaposition of creative elements such as rhythm, melody, and harmony with intellectual aspects of composition, theory, and instrumentation. Like painters mixing red, blue, and yellow into thousands of colors, musicians blend these various elements to create classical symphonies, jazz improvisations, country ballads, and rock-and-roll tunes.

Throughout centuries of musical history, individual musical elements have been blended and modified in infinite ways. The resulting sounds may convey a whole range of moods, emotions, reactions, and messages. Music, then, is both an expression and reflection of human experience and emotion.

The foundations of modern musical styles were laid down by the first ancient musicians who used wood, rocks, animal skins—and their own bodies—to re-create the sounds of the natural world in which they lived. With their hands, their feet, and their very breath they ignited the passions of listeners and moved them to their feet. The dancing, in turn, had a mesmerizing and hypnotic effect that allowed people to transcend their worldly concerns. Through music they could achieve a level of shared experience that could not be found in other forms of communication. For this reason, music has always been part of religious endeavors, from ancient Egyptian religious ceremonies to modern Christian masses. And it has inspired dance movements from kings and queens spinning the minuet to punk rockers slamming together in a mosh pit.

By examining musical genres ranging from Western classical music to rock and roll, readers will find a new understanding of old music and develop an appreciation for new sounds. Books in Lucent's Music Library focus on the music, the musicians, the instruments, and on music's place in cultural history. The songs and artists examined may be easily found in the CD and sheet music collections of local libraries so that readers may study and enjoy the music covered in the books. Informative sidebars, annotated bibliographies, and complete indexes highlight the text in each volume and provide young readers with many opportunities for further discussion and research.

Scene Is Believing

Punk rock music started as a fad and quickly transformed into a global phenomenon that would change the music industry forever. Despite its many changes, punk rock has consistently maintained two important characteristics: It is rock and roll with an upbeat tempo, and it is a movement of the counterculture. A fight against the mainstream, punk rock typically attracted only a handful of listeners. The rest were disgusted or threatened by what they heard or saw and returned to the music played on commercial radio. But those who discovered the significance of punk rock became dedicated and lifelong fans.

Punk rock was unlike mainstream rock. It was formed mostly in small, local communities, or scenes. A scene is a venue, or series of venues, that showcases various bands from the same genre and becomes a meeting place for musicians and fans. Punk rock scenes were small, musicians were accessible, the music was simple and easy to play—and most record labels and music stores wanted nothing to do with it.

Due in part to the controversial nature and radical form of the music, punk rock fans and musicians had to stick together in small communities. They supported each other at live shows, bought each other's records, and formed their own independent record labels and distribution chains. A small and personal group, it was not uncommon to borrow members from other bands and other scenes.

Punk rock has been forever changing and evolving, each new scene a mutation from an earlier scene. The underground rock scene made unconventional music; early punk rock sped up the tempo and spread the scene to new areas. After the first wave of punk rock died out, New Wave took over and began appealing to a wider and more mainstream audience. At the same time, hardcore punk made the tempos more extreme and the rebellion more threatening. Hardcore shows were of-

Patti Smith, one of the key figures on the dynamic New York punk rock scene of the 1970s, performs on stage in 1975 at CBGB, Manhattan's legendary punk club.

Kurt Cobain, seen here performing in 1993, was the front man for the seminal grunge band of the 1990s, Nirvana.

ten dangerous and commonly disrupted by fights or authorities seeking to prevent violence. Post-punk was the artistic and introverted spin-off of punk rock. The music was dark and somber, and bands experimented with new sounds and musical styles.

Gradually, punk rock began to appeal to wider audiences to score commercial success. Many New Wave bands found success, but it was the grunge and pop-punk explosion of the 1990s that saw punk rock achieve its largest audience and most lucrative record sales. Mean-

while, emotional hardcore punk, or emocore, found success, giving hardcore punk surprising personal sentiment. Fans of hardcore were now able to relate to music that was both fervent and heartfelt. As the twentieth century came to a close, a new genre called emo took emocore's lyrics and pop punk's conventional sound to create a massive new subculture for the youth of the new millennium.

Punk rock stunned conservative adults and made for sensational headlines around the world. But most importantly, it appealed to rebellious kids and young adults who were feeling alienated and misunderstood and gave them new friends, bands to cheer on, and styles to wear. Punk rock had started small—just a few bands playing just a few clubs. But just because record executives, political leaders, parents, and other adults initially did not understand the music did not mean it lacked merit. And just because it started in small groups did not mean that punk rock could not change the world.

Chapter One

Underground Rock

Before punk rock became popular in the mid-1970s, underground rock had created many of the core values that punk rockers drew upon to create a new musical genre. *Underground rock* was a term for a style of music that differed greatly from the popular sound of rock and roll of the late 1960s and early 1970s. Sometimes called garage rock, underground rock was not commercially successful, but it would become the stepping-stone to the punk rock movement.

America at Unease

The underground rock scene started in 1965 and was partially a reaction to the political and social crises of the time period. By the mid-1960s the American involvement in Vietnam had become a full-scale war. Clashes with the National Guard and the police at antiwar demonstrations across the United States left some protestors dead. In southern states, African Americans and those sympathetic to their cause held peaceful demonstrations, marches, and sit-ins to fight for equal rights.

At the same time, America was crippled with high unemployment rates and increasing poverty levels. Unemployment in the country reached nearly 7 percent at its height, the average pay for minimum wage was one dollar per hour, and inflation rose to over 5 percent by the end of the decade.

A Rock-and-Roll Rebellion

Music from the underground scene reflected the state of the world in a way many young adults felt was realistic. While some conventional bands used metaphors to sing songs about drug use, underground bands sang openly about drugs. Rather than hopeful messages of the future, underground musicians sang about the end of the world.

Underground rock, with its basic and noncommercial sound, was the opposite of mainstream rock and roll. Some mainstream progressive rock bands like Led Zeppelin and the Grateful Dead were releasing music that featured intricate instrumental work. In contrast, musicians of the underground scene made music that was simple and sometimes even amateurish in sound. The first, and most influential, of these bands was the Velvet Underground.

Formation of the Underground

When musicians Lou Reed and John Cale formed the Velvet Underground in New York City in 1965, it was the beginning of the underground rock scene. Reed, the lead singer of the Velvet Underground, wrote most of the band's music. He came from a middle-class family in Brooklyn. After he graduated college, Reed moved back to New York City, where he met Cale, a classically trained violist, pianist, and composer. The name of the band came from a book written by Michael Leigh about sadomasochism, in which pleasure is derived from emotional and physical pain, a recurring theme in the band's songs.

The Velvets' sound was simple yet original. Their chords were basic, and they utilized strange noises such as heavy distortion, which is a mixture of buzz and static, and Cale's screeching

Armed with fixed bayonets, National Guardsmen surround a large group of peace activists during a 1969 protest against the war in Vietnam.

In 1965 John Cale (front) and Lou Reed (second from rear) formed the Velvet Underground, the most influential band of New York's underground movement.

electric viola. The band played its first two live shows shortly after forming. The first was on November 11, 1965, at a high school in New Jersey, and the second was in December at the Café Bizarre, an ice cream parlor in Manhattan. It was at the second performance that the band's unconventional sound caught the attention of Andy Warhol.

Warhol was a famous Pop Art painter and experimental filmmaker. His art studio, dubbed the Factory, was a center for painters, musicians, filmmakers, and other artists. Reed commented on the band's similarities with Warhol: "Andy Warhol told me that what we were doing with the music was the same thing he was doing with painting and movies and writing—i.e., not kidding around. To my mind nobody in music was doing anything that even approximated the real thing, with the exception of us."[1]

Warhol introduced the band members to a woman named Nico and convinced them to use her as their lead singer. Nico was a German model, actress, and aspiring singer who had come to New York City in search of a musical career. She provided a stunning contrast to the other members of the Velvets. She was a natural beauty: tall, blonde, and always fashionable. While the rest of the band was dressed in all black, she often wore all white.

Sounds from the Underground

Warhol produced the band's first album, titled *The Velvet Underground and Nico*. There were many problems with the release of the record, however, and it spent nearly a year on the shelf at MGM Records. One issue was the controversial lyrics and subject matter contained in songs such as "Heroin," which glamorized drug use and presented a pessimistic view of society and the future. The content of the entire album foreshadowed the punk rock movement with its intentional thematic departure from mainstream sensibilities; it excluded chipper love songs and optimistic messages. It was influential for other musicians who would fuel the underground movement in the following years.

There were many reasons for the Velvet Underground's appeal and influence to the burgeoning movement, including their lack of commercial success. They influenced key figures with their offbeat originality: The lyrical content was extreme and unique, but so were the pace and length of the songs. Songs like "Heroin" and "Chelsea Girls" were more than seven minutes long, and "Sister Ray" was more than seventeen minutes long, nearly one entire side of the record *White Light/White Heat*. Most conventional rock-and-roll songs at the time were between three and five minutes long.

The sound of the music was also distinct. Reed's songs were known for their unpredictable and uneven stanzas, and the band's recordings and live performances featured heavy distortions and massive electronic feedback from

The Velvet Underground performs on stage in a small club in 1966. The band was known for its exceptionally loud and wildly unpredictable live performances.

the amplifiers. The distortion and feedback gave the band an amateurish sound that defied Reed and Cale's formal musical training. But their amateur quality was a deliberate attempt to create unrehearsed and unpolished-sounding music. For most listeners, the resonance was too much. Charles O'Hara of the band Riff Doctors describes a 1968 performance in Pittsburgh: "The sound is loud, driving, and hard. The words are tough, and Lou spits them out in an atonal, vicious manner . . . the volume is ear splitting. A jet plane on stage would not have as profound an effect on the audience, which has by now been reduced by half."[2]

Prolonging the *Inevitable*

Since the Velvet Underground's unorthodox sound had failed to earn widespread success, Warhol created *The Exploding Plastic Inevitable*, a live, multimedia extravaganza that toured for over a year. Despite his attempts to jump-start their career, the band's lineup began to dissolve.

The Velvet Underground's influence at the time, and for years to follow, was vast. Because of them, many young people began to take an interest in the budding underground sound. According to Steve Severin, the bassist for the London punk band Siouxsie and the Banshees, "everyone who listened to the Velvet Underground started a band. . . . I know I did."[3]

When *The Exploding Plastic Inevitable* played in Detroit in late 1967,

two men in particular were inspired enough by the band that they soon helped advance and expand the underground sound. Nate Finkelstein, a

The Exploding Plastic Inevitable

Andy Warhol wanted to make the Velvet Underground the center of a unique sound and light experience. The show he created for the band became an important example of increasing audience participation and blurred the line between the audience and the performers, which would later be a driving force in the punk rock scene. The band performed in its usual manner onstage as lights, mirrored balls, and colored slides lit up the room. Numerous Warhol films played on the walls while dancers intermingled with audience members. During the first few productions, a camera crew filmed interviews with audience members, asking them blunt and sexually explicit questions. Their uncomfortable reactions and responses led to the show's original title, *Andy Warhol, Up-tight*, but the show's name was eventually changed to *The Exploding Plastic Inevitable*. During the show's life span, the Velvet Underground traveled as far west as Los Angeles and San Fran-

cisco and as far north as Ontario, Canada. The show played for more than a year, from its first performance on January 13, 1966, until May of 1967, when the public's exposure to similar mixed-media productions had lessened the show's shocking impact. Despite its short run, the show was essential to the Velvet Underground earning a limited but dedicated following.

Pop artist Andy Warhol (second from right) produced a stage show for the Velvet Underground that incorporated a visual spectacle to complement the music.

Seen here on stage in 1977, Iggy Pop was infamous for his outlandish onstage antics, which included cutting his arms and chest with broken beer bottles.

photographer and a frequenter of Andy Warhol's Factory, said of the show: "Ann Arbor was very important. Iggy Pop was there. That's how he came in contact with the Velvets. They also had a big effect on Wayne Kramer of the MC5, who were also there. You could say everything came from the Velvets."[4]

The Power of Pop

Iggy Pop and the Stooges and MC5 shaped the future sound of punk rock by speeding up the pace of the Velvets' distinct sound and content. Born James Osterberg in the Detroit suburb of Ann Arbor, Iggy Pop got his name from the Iguanas, a band that he played in during high school. After hearing the Velvet Underground, he was inspired to form his own band. Pop described the first time he heard the Velvet Underground: "I just hated the sound. . . . Then, about six months later it hit me. . . . [*The Velvet Underground and Nico*] became very key for me, not just for what it was, and for how good it was, but also because I heard other people who could make good music without being good at music. It gave me hope. . . . The sound was so cheap and yet so good."[5]

Pop's band, named the Psychedelic Stooges, later shortened to the Stooges, formed in 1967. They opened for MC5 at the Grande Ballroom in Detroit the night MC5 recorded *Kick Out the Jams*. By chance, Cale of the Velvet Underground was in attendance and was impressed by the raw energy of Pop's band. A few months later, Cale produced their first album, *The Stooges*.

Like MC5, the Stooges took the Velvet Underground's fondness for unconventional sounds and controversial thematic material to new levels with their ear-piercing guitars and pounding beats. The band even once placed a blender that was half full of water onstage with a microphone above it and turned it on for fifteen minutes before finally beginning its act.

It was Pop's bizarre onstage behavior that made the band notorious, however. As the lead singer, Pop would often wear golf shoes while performing, which would make a unique clacking sound on the wood stage. He was addicted to heavy drugs and alcohol and often performed under their influence. He used glass from broken beer bottles to slash his arms and chest and would bleed all over the stage. He would frequently lose control of his body and would flail violently around the stage and even into the crowd. Pop explained why he moved the way he did to *Rolling Stone* magazine in 1970: "The music drives me into a peak freak. I can't feel any pain or realize what goes on around me, and when I dive into a sea of people, it is the feeling of the music, the mood."[6]

As the band began to dissolve in 1973, British rocker David Bowie decided to help revive Pop's career. Bowie secured a new record deal for the band and convinced Pop to quit drugs, which Pop was able to do for a few years. Bowie produced the band's

MC5 Jams

One of the first bands to gain recognition in Detroit was MC5, short for Motor City Five. The group lived in a commune on the campus of the University of Michigan, located in Ann Arbor, in the suburbs of Detroit. MC5 originally started out in 1964 as a straightforward rock-and-roll band. However, by 1966 the band had decided to incorporate more distortion and electronic feedback into its music, much like the Velvet Underground. Founding member and guitarist Wayne Kramer was in attendance when the Velvet Underground's show, *The Exploding Plastic Inevitable*, performed in Detroit, and he drew much motivation from the show.

On Halloween night of 1968, MC5 headlined a show at the trendy Grande Ballroom. The performance was recorded and became the band's first album, *Kick Out The Jams*. The album was not successful, and MC5's label, Electra Records, dropped the band not long afterward. Despite being short-lived, MC5

had a strong impact on the sound of underground rock. While its music was similar in some aspects to the Velvet Underground's, with its throbbing distortion and controversial anarchical subject matter, the difference was MC5's ferociously rhythmic beat and vigor.

The short-lived group MC5 from Detroit had a profound impact on the sound of underground punk.

1973 release *Raw Power,* which received good critical reviews but was disliked by fans due to its departure from their earlier sound. The Stooges broke up after the album, but Bowie and Pop continued to collaborate for a few more years. Prior to producing *Raw Power,* Bowie had had a much larger impact on the upcoming punk rock movement: glamour rock.

David Bowie and Glam Rock

Born David Jones in London, England, Bowie's first important impact on the underground rock scene came in 1970 when he was pictured on the cover of his second album, *The Man Who Sold the World,* in a dress. Then in May 1972 he released *The Rise and Fall of Ziggy Stardust and the Spiders from Mars,* which chronicled the arrival of a drone named Ziggy Stardust on Earth, his interactions, and in the last song, entitled "Rock and Roll Suicide," his death. Ziggy was an androgynous, or genderless, creature from outer space that had come to Earth to observe its species. While dressed as Ziggy onstage, Bowie would wear tight-fitting, futuristic bodysuits, short and spiky orange hair, and white powder makeup. Many fans mimicked his intentionally poorly dyed hair and his makeup. This style of costume and heavily exaggerated makeup made famous by Bowie was called glamour rock, or glam rock for short. Despite his growing popularity and eventual move into the mainstream, the impact of Bowie's glam rock style continued to flourish in the underground scene.

Bowie's use of the asexual image and of female clothing sparked a movement against conventional dress codes and gender identities. His fans also began dressing ambiguously or as transvestites. Just as important as the image he had created onstage was the fact that Bowie appeared in public in his Ziggy Stardust costume, which in turn caused fans to do the same. This was a distinct departure from the rock scene prior to Ziggy's arrival. It represented a transition from bizarre onstage personalities to the full-fledged public lifestyle that punk would later become.

At the same time that Bowie's Ziggy Stardust character was "alive," Lou Reed had been singing about transvestitism in songs such as 1973's "Walk on the Wild Side," which was about several transvestites he had met at Andy Warhol's Factory. Also around the same time, a transvestite band called the New York Dolls formed and was among the first groups to shape the New York punk rock scene.

Dress-Up Dolls

Originally formed in late 1971, the quintet from Manhattan was initially called Actress. But after replacing guitarist Rick Rivets with Sylvain Sylvain, the band changed its name to the Dolls of New York, then flip-flopped it to the New York Dolls. The other founding members were lead singer David Johansen, guitarist Johnny Thunders, bassist Arthur Kane, and drummer

Billy Murcia. With their unmistakable appearance and high-energy rock, the New York Dolls were in a category all by themselves.

The Dolls shocked their audiences by taking the androgynous look of Bowie's Ziggy Stardust and raising it to a whole new level. Rather than Ziggy's unisex style, the Dolls would wear dresses, spotted leotards, pantyhose, high platform shoes, and long, poufed hair along with heavy makeup and painted fingernails. While performing, Johansen would parody Rolling Stones front man Mick Jagger while Thunders and Sylvain struggled to keep from falling over in their platform boots. Their transvestite look was glam rock at its extreme. Johansen defended their style: "The press figured it was glitter rock—the term itself came from some writer, but it was just classical rock and roll. . . . And we thought that's the way you were supposed to be if you were in a rock and roll band. Flamboyant."[7]

The band was also known for its use of safety pins, which became a key punk rock accessory. According to one insider, the Dolls got most of their dresses from a man named Frenchy, but the dresses were old and frail, so they would tear easily. Frenchy's solution was to use safety pins to keep them together, and the trend took off from there.

It was not just their style that made the Dolls a groundbreaking band; it was their sound as well. They played songs about sex, drugs, and teenage confusion with a simplistic approach to rock that progressive bands had lacked. Critic John Rockwell from *Rolling Stone* explained, "They reaffirmed the Velvet Underground's commitment to amateurish primitivism but proved it could be energetic, dizzying fun and street hard all at once."[8] The Dolls took the Velvets' content, Bowie's look, and Detroit rock's tempo and packaged them all together into one revolutionary band.

Punk Rock Look and Lifestyle

In June 1972 the Dolls began a seventeen-week gig at the Mercer Arts Center in the East Village in lower Manhattan. The Mercer Arts Center was located in the Broadway Central Hotel and consisted of several boutiques and performance areas, including theaters, cabarets, and even the Kitchen, which was actually the hotel's old kitchen, used for video art and experimental music. At Mercer, various artist friends and heroin addicts had supported the Dolls early on, but as word spread on the street of this pioneering new band, people like Bowie, Warhol, and Elton John began showing up at their shows.

Unfortunately for the Dolls, their clothing style, musical content, and self-destructive lifestyles made the record companies shy away from signing them. In fact, during negotiations with record labels in London, drummer Murcia died at a nearby party from a drug overdose. It was not until the Dolls returned to New York and chose

Dressed as the androgynous extraterrestrial Ziggy Stardust, David Bowie performs his trademark glam rock spectacle in London in 1973.

a replacement drummer for Murcia named Jerry Nolan that Mercury Records signed them and released their self-titled debut album in July 1973. They released a second album titled *Too Much Too Soon* less than a year later, in May 1974. Meanwhile, the band faced several problems. Thunders and Nolan both developed heroin addictions, and Kane suffered from alcoholism. Manager Marty Thau felt the band had become uncontrollable and in early 1975 allowed a British fashion boutique owner named Malcolm McLaren to take over.

As the Dolls' new manager, McLaren vowed to freshen up their image and clean up their act. However, he admitted that at the time he knew much less about music than he did about image. McLaren decided to have the Dolls wear red leather outfits with a Com-

With their outrageous costumes and ear-splitting sound, the New York Dolls were one of the most influential forerunners of the Manhattan punk scene of the mid-1970s.

munist sickle and hammer as the backdrop while they played their shows, but American audiences did not care for the new fashion statement and failed to understand that the band was not sincerely supporting communism. The Dolls split up in April 1975 during a tour of Florida.

Despite their brief three-year existence, the New York Dolls were unmistakably important to the emerging punk rock scene. Johansen modestly summed up their significance by saying, "I think what the Dolls did as far as being an influence on punk was that we showed that anybody could do it."[9] But *Rolling Stone* critic Rockwell supports this claim and goes even further: "The Dolls can lay legitimate claim to being the direct precursors of the mid-seventies New York punk scene. . . . In the heyday of glitter rock, they were most striking at first for their looks— deliberately, poutingly androgynous. But sexual ambivalence wasn't really central to the Dolls' act; music and spirit were."[10]

The Dolls played a major part in inspiring and unifying punk rock fans. People who had attended their shows and listened to their albums religiously began forming their own bands. They had witnessed how the combination of simple compositions, bizarre originality, and a dedicated fan base could turn any band into a spectacle. When the Dolls broke up in April 1975, the New York punk rock scene had already begun to take off, and much of it was because of them.

Chapter Two

New York, New York

In the early 1970s, New York City became the first place that punk rock bands began performing together in the same place, and it was where the sound of punk rock was created. Underground rock bands had influenced new musicians, and once these new musicians were given a place to centralize, the scene began to thrive.

Much like the underground movement that splintered out of mainstream rock in the 1960s, punk rock bands of the 1970s also competed against a more popular rock style. The British Invasion, which brought popular British bands like the Rolling Stones, The Beatles, and The Who to American audiences, had overshadowed underground rock during the 1960s but died out by the time the Beatles disbanded in 1970. Taking the place of the short, catchy songs by the British bands were lengthy and musically complex progressive rock songs. Progressive rock bands such as Led Zeppelin, Pink Floyd, and Yes were popu-

lar in the early 1970s throughout the entire world, while pioneers of the punk rock movement rarely obtained popularity outside of New York City.

In a section of lower Manhattan, punk rock became prevalent. It was here that the term *punk*, meaning a worthless, disrespectful youth or a piece of trash, was first applied to the genre and its fans. Extreme clothing styles borrowed from the underground movement became more pronounced than ever before. Area clubs were designated for punk rock acts. And as for the music itself, it had taken on the controversial and sometimes politically charged messages from the underground sound and had sped up the beat while maintaining the same amateur quality. It was due to New York City's unique circumstances that punk rock found its first of many identities.

Living in the Big Apple

In New York City, much of the middle- and upper-class white population had

LOWER MANHATTAN'S PUNK SCENE

Park Avenue

42nd Street

First Avenue

23rd Street

Broadway

MAX'S KANSAS CITY

MERCER ARTS CENTER

CBGB

East Village

SoHo

Canal Street

Bowery

Houston Street

Tribeca

Franklin Roosevelt Drive

East River

NEW JERSEY

Bronx

Manhattan

NEW YORK

Brooklyn

Staten Island

Atlantic Ocean

Area Shown

left the boroughs of Brooklyn, the Bronx, and parts of Queens and relocated to Staten Island, Long Island, and suburban New Jersey. The term for this phenomenon was *white flight*, which was the movement by large percentages of wealthy, white families away from large cities and into surrounding suburban areas after World War II. Legs McNeil, cofounder of the fanzine *Punk,* describes the metropolitan area in the early 1970s: "It was the end of the white flight . . . people were really leaving New York, and it was kind of deserted, and you really got this feeling that, you know, the parents had left, and you could take over and do whatever you want."[11] In an issue of *New York Magazine*, McNeil writes that the city "was everything an 18-year-old boy could hope for — New York City was about saying yes to everything . . . to reinventing yourself according to your fantasy."[12]

The first clubs to open their doors to unsigned punk rock bands and their fans were located in the seedy and rundown neighborhoods of Tribeca, SoHo, and the East Village. At that time the other venues in New York City, such as the Bottom Line, the Palladium, and the Beacon Theatre, required the performers to be signed to major record labels. But at these new Manhattan clubs, fans of underground and garage rock created the first punk rock community.

KC in NYC

Opened in December 1965 as a bar and hangout spot by a restaurateur named Mickey Ruskin, Max's Kansas City was the place to be in New York during the late 1960s. Located in the East Village on Park Avenue, Max's was frequented by famous artists, actors, musicians, and politicians. Warhol, who was often spotted there with his entourage, described the scene:

> Max's Kansas City was the exact spot where Pop Art and Pop Life came together in the sixties — teenyboppers and sculptors, rock stars and poets from St. Mark's Place, Hollywood actors, checking out what the underground actors were all about, boutique owners and models, modern dancers and go-go dancers — everybody went to Max's and everything got homogenized there.[13]

Bowie described an historic first encounter at Max's: "I met Iggy Pop at Max's Kansas City in 1970 or 1971. Me, Iggy, and Lou Reed at one table with absolutely nothing to say to each other, just looking at each other's eye makeup.[14]

Eventually, Max's began to lose its hip image and its important clientele. Celebrities were being replaced by local punks who were there to see their favorite bands perform. Ruskin watched his club transform from Pop Art to punk throughout the 1970s and decided to shut down Max's in the 1980s. The building still remains today, although it is now a deli.

A man peers into the window of CBGB, the Manhattan club that launched the careers of many of the best-known punk bands of the 1970s.

With the Mercer Arts Center and Max's Kansas City shut down, unsigned bands began looking for another place to play. What they found was a bar a few blocks away called CBGB.

Country, Bluegrass, Blues, and Punk

Located at 315 Bowery in the East Village, CBGB opened in December 1973 and was originally intended by its owner, Hilly Kristal, to be a venue for country, blues, and folk music. Its full abbreviation was CBGB & OMFUG, which stood for Country, Bluegrass, and Blues and Other Music for Uplifting Gormandizers. A gormandizer is a

person who gorges him- or herself, in this instance with music. The bar was part of a flophouse for derelicts and recently released prisoners, most of whom were alcoholics, drug addicts, and criminals. The area surrounding CBGB was called the Bowery and was known for its cheap housing and rundown living conditions. Ramones drummer Tommy Ramone later said that "in the early 1970's New York was empty, there were no clubs. The reason we played CBGBs was that there was no place to play."[15]

Kristal had intended CBGB to showcase country and folk music because he believed that those genres were popular enough to make the club profitable. He soon ran out of original country and blues talent and, starting in early 1974, allowed rock bands to play at his club. Although he did not like their sound, he instituted a new rule: that only rock bands with original music could play at his club. Hundreds of local bands began to surface from all around the area, seeking stage time.

Much like underground rock, the scene at CBGB lent itself to the creation of a new genre of rock by being the opposite of the typical rock-and-roll environment. The small size of the club and stage allowed audience members to interact with the performers. Musicians walked around the crowd before and after sets. And since none of them were famous, they were completely accessible to their fans, unlike rock-and-roll superstars.

The CBGB Rock Festival

During the summer of 1975, Kristal sought to create more exposure for the club and its bands by creating the CBGB Rock Festival. It was intended to showcase the top forty unsigned New York rock bands, and the turnout from the press was substantial. The festival ran from July 16 to August 3 and featured approximately seventy bands instead of the advertised forty.

The goal was to create as much publicity as possible, and many of the bands played twice. The more popular bands that played included the Ramones, Television, and the Heartbreakers. The press, which had previ-

CBGB owner Hilly Kristal originally envisioned his club as a showcase for Manhattan's lively country and folk music scene.

ously ignored CBGB and the local scene, was now touting its praises and acknowledging the talent of these previously undiscovered bands. Locals also showed up in large numbers, and many of them became regulars to the scene soon after.

Around the same time, Max's Kansas City reopened its doors following ownership issues and began booking unsigned bands as well. It was at this point that the scene that was once called street rock—underground and garage rock before that—became punk rock. Writers and photographers came to the clubs more often, and slowly, more and more record labels began showing interest.

Punk Rock Poetry

The first CBGB artist to find success was Patti Smith. As a contributing music journalist for the music magazine *Creem*, a painter, an actress, and an accomplished poet, Smith became known as the Queen of Punk Rock. Smith had tried acting and writing but knew that she really wanted to sing.

In the winter of 1974, Smith began performing at Max's Kansas City by reading her poetry with guitarist Lenny Kaye playing in the background. As her readings became more popular, she added a bass player, a drummer, and a pianist to complete her band. They called themselves the Patti Smith Group. The band's first single featured two tracks: the first was called "Piss Factory," a poem about a New Jersey assembly line worker, and the second was a cover of Jimi Hendrix's "Hey Joe."

Patti Smith, seen here on stage at CBGB in 1978, was the club's first act to achieve a degree of commercial success.

In the spring of 1975, the Patti Smith Group became the first punk rock and CBGB band to be signed to a label, Arista Records. The band released its first album, *Horses*, produced by former Velvet Underground bassist Cale, in December 1975. The album was a great critical success and is considered one of the best rock-and-roll debut albums ever. Smith continued to play at CBGB, though less frequently, and put out three more albums during the 1970s that continued her moderate success.

The Patti Smith Group had demonstrated to fellow punk rockers and their fans that there was a future for their music. Soon after, an avalanche of New York bands would follow in the poet's footsteps. One of them was a band she had headlined with at CBGB named Television.

Television's Set

Formerly known as the Neon Boys, Television had the distinction of being the first punk rock band to play at CBGB. When Television auditioned, they were loud and unorganized; Kristal hated their sound. Even so, after much convincing he allowed them to return to play a show with an unknown band named the Ramones.

Again Kristal did not like the sound of these two bands, and he considered the Ramones to be even more intolerable and inept than Television. Despite this, he decided to take a risk and shift his club away from country and blues and into this new direction. Television performed often at CBGB in the following year, playing a mixture of songs written by guitarists Tom Verlaine and Richard Hell. Eventually, Verlaine had the band primarily playing his own music, which led to Hell's departure in 1975.

The band replaced Hell and moved forward, releasing *Marquee Moon* in May 1977 and *Adventure* in 1978, both on Electra Records. Television's debut album, *Marquee Moon*, has since been honored by *Rolling Stone* as one of the top 150 rock-and-roll albums ever made. The band's sound was defined by the complex dueling guitar work of Verlaine and Richard Lloyd, which eventually led to the birth of New Wave.

Glitter Backlash and the Ramones

As the band that shared the stage with Television for CBGB's second-ever punk rock show, the Ramones quickly raised eyebrows. The group stripped its sound, appearance, and performance down to the bare bones and became instantly influential among scene kids in New York and London. Surrounded by the flamboyant fashion of the New York Dolls and the artful poems of the Patti Smith Group, the Ramones stood out with their look of solidarity and simple, four-chord songs.

John Cummings, Jeff Hyman, and Douglas Colvin formed the band in January 1974 in the New York borough of Queens. Colvin had begun hanging out with Hyman because of their similar taste in music. According to Colvin, "Maybe three people liked the Stooges in the whole area. And everybody else was violently against them. So if you liked the Stooges you had to be friends with each other."[16] All three were unremarkable musical talents, and Colvin could not sing and play guitar at the same time. This led their manager, Tommy Erdley, to suggest a lineup change, which actually involved him becoming part of the band.

The Ramones next adopted a style, wearing ragged, black-leather jackets, tattered T-shirts, torn jeans, sneakers, and long, black hair. Their look helped

The Ramones

The Ramones became known for having a distinct stage presence. Many times they played their songs so fast that they would either finish a set in twenty minutes or play songs over again to fill time. When they played overseas in the United Kingdom on July 4, 1976, at the Roundhouse in London, the audience included members of the Clash, the Sex Pistols, and the Misfits, all of whom were greatly inspired by the Ramones. Despite playing to large crowds in the United Kingdom, the Ramones continued to get very little attention from American audiences. After a concert at the Palladium in New York on January 7, 1978, *New York Times* rock columnist Robert Palmer criticized their performance: "Their set was monotonous as usual. It is difficult to believe that people have formed serious intellectual attachments to the Ramones and consider their music great or even good rock-and-roll. . . . They are the kind of joke that one tires of rapidly."

Although the Ramones were very popular in the United Kingdom, American audiences initially found the New York band unappealing.

Quoted in Robert Palmer, "Rock: The Ramones." *New York Times,* January 9, 1978, p. C27.

spark the so-called glitter backlash, in which many performers and fans created similar styles. The Ramones also pretended to be dumb teenagers to earn street credibility. Finally, they all went by the surname of Ramone, which was an assumed name used by Beatle Paul McCartney early in his career, and either used their own first names or stage names. The band's original lineup featured Hyman as Joey on vocals, Cummings as Johnny on bass guitar, Colvin as Dee Dee on guitar, and Erdley as Tommy on the drums.

During their early shows, the Ramones would argue onstage about which songs to play next. Their inadequate talent affected the types of songs that they wrote and played, which were usually three- or four-chord pieces, repeated over and over and with a notable lack of instrumental solos. The songs were short and very upbeat; their lyrics were amateurish, with oft-recurring choruses. But their crude sound led to many Ramones fans forming their own bands and to many others emulating their style.

The Blitzkrieg Sound

During the CBGB Rock Festival, the Ramones were one of the featured

The Ramones, shown here in concert in 1979, continued to perform until 1996.

bands. This helped lead to their signing with Sire Records a few months later. In April 1976 Sire released their self-titled debut album, which only took eighteen hours to record. The album featured fourteen songs but had a running time of only twenty-nine minutes. *The Ramones* featured punk rock anthems such as "Blitzkrieg Bop," "Judy Is a Punk," and "I Wanna Be Your Boyfriend." Joe Strummer, lead singer of the Clash, explained the album's importance: "It can't be stressed how great the Ramones' first album was to the scene in London. It was simple enough to be able to play. Me and Paul [Simonon, the Clash bassist] would definitely spend hours, days, weeks, playing along to the record."[17]

Soon after, drummer Erdley left the band to escape the rigors of touring, and the position of drummer became a revolving door for the Ramones. Despite their numerous lineup changes and a longstanding personal and political feud between Hyman and Cummings, the Ramones continued to play until 1996. They had been together for twenty-two years, released fourteen studio albums and five live albums, and played 2,263 shows. They were inducted into the Rock and Roll Hall of Fame in 2002 and remain one of the most influential punk rock bands in history.

Debbie Harry Is Blondie
Less influential but more commercially successful than the Ramones was the band Blondie, fronted by the stun-ningly beautiful Debbie Harry. Harry's gorgeous looks combined with her striking soprano voice seemingly made her an odd fit for the early punk rock movement. Nevertheless, Blondie was able to transcend the punk rock genre and reinvent its sound in nearly every one of its early releases.

Blondie received its first recording contract from Private Stock Records in late 1975 and released its first album, *Blondie*, in December 1976. The album was unsuccessful, and the band's contract was sold to Chrysalis Records, who re-released the album along with Blondie's second album, *Plastic Letters*, in late 1977. This new record was much more successful, scoring two top-ten singles, "Denis (Denee)" and "(I'm Always Touched by Your) Presence, Dear." To support the record, the band toured America opening for Bowie and Pop and eventually became massively successful during the New Wave phenomenon.

Art-School Art Punk
The Ramones may have been the most influential to punk rock's sound, and Blondie may have been the most commercially successful New York punk band, but the Talking Heads were arguably the most popular band among the scene kids. They preferred not to be called punk rockers; their music has been referred to as New Wave, art punk, intellectual rock, or as Kristal likened them, "the Bach of rock and roll."[18] Drummer Chris Franz supports their claim against being a punk rock

Debbie Harry enjoyed tremendous commercial success as the singer for the punk/New Wave band Blondie.

The Talking Heads, pictured on stage in New York's Central Park, helped define the New Wave sound that became wildly popular in the 1980s.

band: "The big difference between us and punk groups is that we like K.C. and the Sunshine Band and Funkadelic/Parliament. You ask [Sex Pistol's] Johnny Rotten if he likes K.C. and the Sunshine Band and he'll blow snot in your face."[19]

Franz, David Byrne, and Tina Weymouth, the founding members of the Talking Heads, all attended art school together at the Rhode Island School of Design in the early 1970s. They practiced for six months before they played their first show at CBGB as the Talking Heads in March 1975. Their first regular gig was opening for the Ramones at CBGB. Their early sound was thin; Weymouth's bass lines formed the backbone of most songs, with the guitar and drums kept to a minimum. But the band came to desire a fuller sound and added keyboardist Jerry Harrison in 1976.

Byrne-ing Down the House

It was Byrne, the band's front man, who quickly became the reason most fans became fascinated by the Talking Heads. He dressed conservatively, looked nerdy, and did not seem to fit the rock-and-roll image. In a 1977 article, the British magazine *New Musical Express* described Byrne as a "tense looking man who folds his arms, tucking his hands in as if he was in a straightjacket."[20] He had a distinct

The Fate of CBGB

Hilly Kristal and CBGB continues to operate into the twenty-first century, but only a few years after the CBGB Rock Festival, the original scene began to change. After a while it became unrealistic to feature only unsigned bands, with the emergence of independent record labels and the growing popularity of the club. In 2005 the landlords of the building in which the club is located escalated the rent to an amount Kristal was no longer able to pay and CBGB would be closed down in 2006. Several popular rock bands, such as the Circle Jerks, the Misfits, the Offspring, and Thursday, hosted benefit shows in an attempt to save the landmark venue. Even without a lease, Kristal continued to run the club and managed to book bands several months in advance. Typical of the rebellious genre that it spawned, CBGB and its management remained defiant.

voice, high, neurotic, and with nodal limitations. His songwriting skills were notable for their simplicity and naïveté.

After opening for the Ramones early on, the Talking Heads began to headline their own shows. They were a regular at CBGB and became the most popular band there, selling out shows constantly for two years. Their large audiences consisted of college students, friends from school, and music critics. In 1977 they signed with Sire Records. Their first studio album was *Talking Heads: 77,* released in September 1977. They toured Europe in support of their record with label mates the Ramones. Upon returning they recorded and released *More Songs About Buildings and Food* in July 1978, which brought them moderate success.

Like Blondie and Television, the Talking Heads were another New York band credited with creating the New Wave sound that would become popular in the early 1980s. In 2002, the band played together for the last time when it was inducted into the Rock and Roll Hall of Fame. It was a fitting way to go; for among the artists the Talking Heads were inducted with that day were fellow Sire Records alumni and the band they had first opened for, the Ramones.

The Blank Generation

Despite the number of groundbreaking bands produced, one of early punk rock's biggest aesthetic influences came from one man, Richard Hell, a former member of the Neon Boys and Television. A mere six days after the tremendously influential New York Dolls broke up, Hell formed a band with former Dolls guitarist Thunders and drummer Nolan. They called themselves the Heartbreakers.

Hell himself had stood out in the punk rock scene in the same way that the Dolls had stood out in the underground rock scene. He had black, spiky hair and wore studded dog collars and torn-up shirts mended with safety pins. When the Heartbreakers played at the CBGB Rock Festival in July 1975, former Dolls manager and London boutique owner McLaren was in the audience. McLaren was shocked and delighted by Hell's style in the same way that he had been struck by the Dolls' outlandish and unique fashion in London when he'd first seen them. Like he had with the Dolls, McLaren asked Hell if he would travel back to London with him to form a band. Hell declined his offer.

Not long after, Hell left the Heartbreakers and formed another band, Richard Hell and the Voidoids, which included the future Marky Ramone, Marc Bell, on drums. The band signed with punk rock mainstay Sire Records and released its first album, *Blank Generation*, in 1977. The title track became an anthem for punk rockers in New York and even a label for the era, with its nihilistic lyrics and stark negativity. Hell had left high school and moved from Kentucky to New York to become a poet. With the exception of Smith, Hell was considered the most poetic and intelligent of the New York songwriters.

Richard Hell and the Voidoids became a popular act at CBGB, and they traveled to England to open for the popular British punk rock band the Clash. Meanwhile, McLaren had returned to his boutique in West London with the notion to form a punk rock group in Richard Hell's image. The band would become the groundbreaking Sex Pistols.

Chapter Three

London Calling

Every development that underground, glamour, street, and punk rock all made in the ten years between the formation of the Velvet Underground and the rise of CBGB was leading straight to London. Between 1976 and 1979, punk rock in its truest form lived in the United Kingdom.

There were several reasons why punk rock matured and died in London. In terms of controversy, punk rock reached its pinnacle in the United Kingdom. Fans became rabid supporters of their favorite groups and at times became menaces to society. The punk rock fashion borrowed from everything before it, from transvestitism to safety pins, and became a uniform for scene kids. Also, the politics of punk rock began to take shape in the form of anarchism. But above all else, big-name bands like the Sex Pistols and the Clash became sensations at home and overseas. Like New York City, the turmoil in London helped shape the new punk rock movement.

A Tale of Two Cities

As bad as problems were in America, they had become much worse in the United Kingdom. The unemployment rate in the mid-1970s was higher than it had been at any point since the end of World War II. Living expenses were increasing, leaving many people struggling to make ends meet and many others on the British welfare system known as the dole.

The problems seemed to be most difficult for members of the younger generation. Most of them were on the dole and received minimal checks from the government. Their future seemed bleak, and they were growing increasingly disillusioned with their roles in society. Their fear of eternal poverty and their cynicism toward the future served as major igniters of the punk rock scene. All of these issues surfaced in the music, fashion, and lifestyles of punk bands and their followers.

The scenes of New York and London differed greatly. Members of the

New York bands and fan base were generally in their mid-twenties, whereas most of the Londoners were only teenagers. Along with the age gap, there was also a dissimilar type of class struggle. Tricia Henry, author of the book *Break All the Rules*, explains the variation: "The [American] underground-rock movement consisted primarily of middle-class youths rejecting middle-class values. In Britain, punk generally represented working-class youths reacting to the bourgeois status quo."[21] Her claim is best supported by the fact that the New York punk rockers had taken on the "blank generation" slogan, while Londoners used the more depressing and concerning motto of "no future."

The Return of McLaren

After Hell had refused to accompany McLaren back to the United Kingdom, McLaren returned to London alone, but with a concept for a new rock group. Along with his business partner Vivienne Westwood, McLaren ran a clothing boutique on King's Road in West London that specialized in extreme fashions aimed at avant-garde rock stars and their fans. The boutique was famous for its constant name changes, which included Sex; Let It Rock; and Too Fast to Live, Too Young to Die.

Back in 1973, when the store was known as Let It Rock, musicians Paul Cook, Steve Jones, and Wally Nightingale offered McLaren a chance to be the manager of their band, the

A large crowd of punk fans at a 1977 outdoor festival in London poses for the camera as they wait for the next band to take the stage.

With their lewd onstage behavior and their song lyrics that glorified chaos, the Sex Pistols epitomized the attitudes of the English punk scene.

Swankers, but he declined. A few years later, after swapping instruments and replacing Nightingale with bassist Glen Matlock, the band began its search for a lead singer. Again they went to McLaren, who suggested that the band try out a local kid named John Lydon. Lydon had caught McLaren's attention when he walked in the store wearing a homemade T-shirt that read: "I hate Pink Floyd." Matlock, Cook, and Jones held an audition for Lydon in the shop, having him sing along to Alice Cooper songs from the jukebox. Lydon was sneering and intense, and the band offered him a place as the front man. He accepted and took the name Johnny

Rotten, due to his crooked and discolored teeth.

Here's the Sex Pistols

The group named itself the Sex Pistols. Every member of the band, including future bassist Sid Vicious, had criminal records, the longest belonging to Jones. He was an accomplished cat burglar who had even stolen most of the band's original equipment, including microphones, guitars, and an amp from Bowie's final Ziggy Stardust show.

The Pistols encouraged a violent form of participation between the audience and themselves. They were constantly swearing onstage, spitting on the audience and encouraging them to spit on them in return, fighting those who came onstage, and diving into the crowd to combat hecklers. At their shows both sides threw glasses, beer bottles, and chairs at each other.

As the front man, Rotten would sneer and scream his words into the microphone while thrusting around. He would snarl and stare psychotically wide-eyed into the crowd. In terms of his appearance, he looked much like Hell. He had wildly spiked hair and wore old clothes filled with tears and covered with safety pins. He dyed his hair bright colors such as orange and green like Ziggy Stardust.

EMI Records Abandons the Pistols

In November 1975 the Sex Pistols started out playing at small colleges and art schools, then at the few punk rock clubs in London. The most popular club during punk rock's early years was the 100 Club, where the Pistols began playing regularly in 1976. The 100 Club put up with the band's excessive volume, outrageous antics, and unruly fans. EMI Records decided to take a chance on the raucous band and signed the Pistols in October 1976.

The band's signing with EMI marked its first conflict with record sales. EMI released its only Sex Pistols' single, "Anarchy in the U.K.," on November 26, 1976, but the song and the band's promotion for it became immensely controversial. Groups and assemblies all across the United King-

dom spoke out against the shocking and dangerous lyrics, which advocated chaos, and church leaders denounced it. Even though the song managed to peak at number thirty-eight on the U.K. charts, EMI began to withdraw its support of the band.

It soon became clear that the partnership between the Pistols and EMI was near its end. Radio stations banned "Anarchy in the U.K.," and most record stores refused to sell it. Even workers at EMI's Hayes record factory refused to handle the record. EMI had cut tour funding, and local authorities shut down the majority of the *Anarchy Tour* featuring the Pistols, the Clash, the Heartbreakers, and fellow British punk rockers the Damned and the Buzzcocks. On January 6, 1977, EMI announced that it had terminated its contract with the Sex Pistols and gave them considerable severance pay less than two months after their signing.

A Vicious Addition

Approximately one month after EMI abandoned the group, bassist Matlock decided to leave the band. His replacement was Rotten's close friend and the ultimate Sex Pistols' fan John Simon Ritchie, who took the stage name of Sid Vicious. Vicious had previously played in two other groups, Flowers of Romance and Siouxsie and the Banshees, but he really had no musical talent. In the studio, Jones recorded most of the bass lines, and during shows Vicious's bass amp was oftentimes not even turned on.

Unwholesome Television

Many fans had become vocal in their concern that the Sex Pistols had sold out by signing with a major record label. But their concerns were soon quashed. On December 1, 1976, the band made an appearance on the British talk show the *Today Show,* hosted by Bill Grundy. Both Grundy and members of the band appeared to be intoxicated during the interview. Grundy began to taunt the rockers and asked them to "say something outrageous." Several members of the band complied, including Jones and Rotten, who used expletives. By the next morning, newspapers and tabloids had the incident on the front page, including the famous *Daily Mirror* headline: "The Filth and the Fury!"

The situation had become an instant uproar. Grundy was suspended for two weeks immediately following the broadcast. Under their sensational headline, the *Daily Mirror* reported that a man named James Holmes had destroyed his television set while watching the show to protect his eight-year-old son. He was quoted saying: "It blew up and I was knocked backwards. I was so angry and disgusted with this filth that I took a swing with my boot. . . . I don't want this sort of muck coming into my home at teatime."

Quoted in Ed Ward, Geoffrey Stokes, and Ken Tucker, *Rock of the Ages*, New York: Simon and Schuster, 1986, p. 557.

What Vicious lacked in musical talent he made up for in image. Like Rotten, Vicious greatly resembled Hell. He had long, spiky, black hair and was pale and slender. He wore torn-up old clothes and a trademark chain around his neck fastened by a small lock. He often performed live in bondage attire or shirtless, displaying scars and occasionally fresh wounds. He used broken glass bottles to cut his chest before, during, and after his shows and sometimes performed covered in his own blood. He also had a mean streak and was known for his tendency to get into fights.

Royal Pain

A month after Vicious joined the Sex Pistols, the band signed with A&M Records in March 1977. As a publicity stunt, executives staged the signing of the new contract in front of Buckingham Palace to coincide with the release of the Pistols' new single "God Save the Queen," which became their next major controversy. Despite A&M pressing twenty-five thousand copies of the single, high-level record executives, fearing bad publicity, decided to terminate the contract a mere week after its signing, paying out yet another severance check. Most copies of the A&M single were incinerated, but those not destroyed are now among the most valuable vinyl records in the world.

The Pistols signed what would be their final record contract with Virgin Records in early May 1977. The label had to settle a dispute with factory workers who, like EMI workers, refused to handle the controversial single. Finally, "God Save the Queen" was released on May 27 at the height of Queen Elizabeth II's Silver Jubilee celebration, a British tradition of honoring a monarch's twenty-fifth anniversary on the throne. The timing and naturally divisive lyrics turned the song into a huge scandal. The song also ended with Rotten repeating "there's no future" over and over, which became a London punk rock rally cry.

On the album sleeve was an illustration of Elizabeth with a safety pin through her lip, which was considered borderline blasphemy. To top off the controversy, on the biggest day of the celebration, the Pistols performed from a boat on the River Thames as it passed by the Houses of Parliament. Police forces arrived on boats, attacked the passengers, and arrested the band.

During a 1977 Sex Pistols show, Johnny Rotten screams into the microphone alongside bassist Sid Vicious, who has sliced up his chest with a razor.

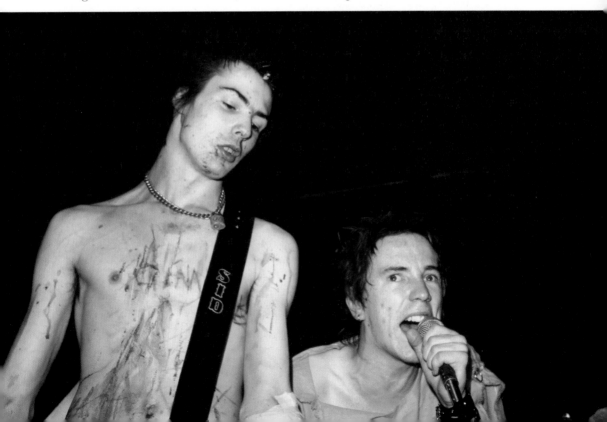

"God Save the Queen" managed to anger nearly every authority figure and most citizens. Members of the Pistols fell victim to brutal attacks. Rotten was assaulted by a National Front group loyal to the queen, and Cook was also attacked and nearly scalped the next day. The song was quickly banned from the airwaves, and its availability in record stores was limited. On the British top-twenty singles chart Top of the Pops, an empty box was used to represent the song, which peaked at number two despite speculation that it had actually outsold the number one single, Rod Stewart's "The First Cut Is the Deepest," but was left out of the top position for political reasons.

No More Nonsense

After much anticipation, stifling controversy, and a total of four successful singles, *Never Mind the Bollocks, Here's the Sex Pistols* was released by Virgin Records on October 28, 1977. It was the Pistols' first and only official album. It included the smash hits "Anarchy in the U.K." and "God Save the Queen" along with their latest top-ten singles, "Pretty Vacant" and "Holiday in the Sun." The album sold massively in the United Kingdom, reaching number one on the charts. It received much critical acclaim, including being voted as the best album of the year by the critics of the *Village Voice* and being named as the second most influential album of the previous twenty years by *Rolling Stone*.

Musically, nearly every song on the album is as dissonant as the next. The first track, "Holiday in the Sun," written by the Pistols while they were in Berlin to escape the bad press in the United Kingdom, is about a Nazi concentration camp and a longing to go under the Berlin Wall to the Communist East side. Billie Joe Armstrong, front man of the pop-punk group Green Day, wrote in a 2004 tribute to the band: "The things that Lydon wrote about back in '76 and '77 are totally relevant to what's going on right now. They paint an ugly picture. No one ever had the guts to say what they said . . . the only person who did anything similar to it was Bob Dylan, and even Bob Dylan was never that blunt."[22]

Following the success of *Never Mind the Bollocks*, the Pistols began what would be their final tour. The two-week American tour was a nightmare. They faced several cancellations, hostile crowds, illness, and exhaustion. Vicious was attacked by audience members in the South and even by his own bodyguards.

During the final show of the tour in San Francisco on January 14, 1978, Rotten turned his back on the band and the audience. "Ever get the feeling you've been cheated?"[23] he asked as he walked offstage. Three days later Rotten announced that the band had broken up.

Following the breakup of the Sex Pistols, McLaren sold his boutique and found success as a solo artist in the 1990s. Cook and Jones continued to work together on the soundtrack for

Following the breakup of the Sex Pistols, Johnny Rotten formed a post-punk group known as Public Image Ltd., seen here performing in 1988.

the Pistols' documentary, *The Great Rock 'n' Roll Swindle*, released in 1979. The soundtrack featured a combination of previously unreleased Pistols' tracks, orchestral versions of "God Save the Queen" and "EMI," and songs by acquaintances. Rotten reverted to his given name, John Lydon, formed the post-punk band Public Image Ltd., and released two moderately successful albums. The Pistols reunited to play shows in 1996, 2002, and 2003. They were ultimately inducted into the Rock and Roll Hall of Fame in March 2006.

Dressed to Unimpress

Famous punk rockers such as Rotten and Vicious were great examples of the wild fashions that swept through London. Although torn T-shirts and jeans and the safety pin look were made popular by the New York bands, this look became common in London because many youths could not afford to buy expensive clothes anyway.

In the United Kingdom, punk rockers began to take the style even further. They used safety pins, chains, and razor blades as jewelry, even piercing cheeks and ears with safety pins. The

Sid and Nancy

After the dissolution of the Sex Pistols, bassist Sid Vicious met up with girlfriend Nancy Spungen in New York to pursue a solo career. His only album, *Sid Sings*, was released by Virgin Records in December 1979. It featured three top-ten singles in the United Kingdom, including a punk rock version of Frank Sinatra's "My Way."

But one year earlier, on the morning of October 12, 1978, Spungen was found dead on the bathroom floor with a single stab wound to her stomach. The police arrested Vicious and charged him with her murder. Vicious and Spungen were both heavy heroin users, and Vicious claimed he was in a drugged daze at the time of Spungen's death and had no recollection of the event. While in prison, Vicious was put into drug rehabilitation. He was then released on bail money posted by Virgin Records at the request of former Sex Pistols manager Malcolm McLaren. During a party to celebrate his temporary release from prison, Vicious overdosed on a pure form of heroin and died the next day, February 2, 1979. John Lydon was not surprised by Vicious's fate: "He was very influenced by the New York thing, like the Lou Reed culture, where heroin was presented as a glorious lifestyle of fun and decadence. And he childishly believed all that."

During a heroin-induced frenzy in 1978, Sid Vicious stabbed and killed his girlfriend Nancy Spungen.

Quoted in *Sex Pistols: Never Mind the Bollocks*. DVD. Directed by Matthew Longfellow. Los Angeles, CA: Isis Productions, 2002.

Mohawk, or Mohican in the United Kingdom, became a popular hairstyle, with the hair short on the sides and long and usually spiked down the center. Makeup and brightly dyed hair came from the glam rock movement. Phrases and band names were often written on or painted onto clothing. Bondage clothing made out of leather, rubber, and vinyl also became popular due to its connotations with sexual deviancy.

Fashion was also influenced by the movement against assumptions based on appearance. This concept first appeared with Bowie's space character Ziggy Stardust, whose asexual appearance was an attempt to blur gender lines. Underground rockers had sought to destroy social conventions by proving the old cliché that you cannot judge a book by its cover. Examples of this in the punk rock scene included the wearing of neckties and Doc Martens boots, because both were associated with the workplace and most punk rockers were unemployed.

Many of the punk rock styles, such as Nazi swastikas, were worn for shock value or to send a message. As a whole, the London punk rock scene was not racist. Punk rockers aligned themselves against neo-Nazis and their organizations, which led to numerous violent clashes between the groups. Sid Vicious often wore a bright red Swastika shirt and wrote the song "Belsen Was a Gas" about the concentration camp Bergen-Belsen purely for shock value. Scene kids used the Nazi

This Londoner's dress, with his bright red shoes and outrageous jewelry, was typical of the English punk scene.

imagery to remind citizens of the horrors of fascism, which they believed the British government was heading toward.

Revolution Rockers

Another British band that sought to warn youths about the dangers of fascism was the Clash. While the Sex Pistols sang about nihilism and anarchy and sought the destruction of rock and roll, as one of their counterparts and tour mates, the Clash achieved more commercial success in its moderation. In contrast to the Pistols' blatant excesses, the Clash mixed genres to create its own niche in rock while also tackling feasible social problems. Rather than the shocking stance of "Anarchy in the U.K.," the Clash released "Career Opportunities" about burgeoning unemployment. The band fused punk rock with reggae, ska, and blues to form a unique sound that enabled it to find mainstream success by the early 1980s and cement its legendary status.

When the Pistols played in London on April 3, 1976, in support for the rock band the 101ers, they grabbed the attention of the 101ers' lead singer, Joe Strummer, who decided to leave his band and become part of the punk movement "five seconds into [the Pistols'] first song."[24] He joined up with guitarist Mick Jones and bassist Paul Simonon, members of London SS, yet another allusion to Nazi Germany. Strummer, Jones, and Simonon added drummer Terry Chimes and guitarist Keith Levene, who did not last long and eventually joined Rotten's post-Pistols band, Public Image Ltd. McLaren convinced his former business partner and Clash manager Bernie Rhodes to have the band open for the Pistols beginning in the summer of 1976.

Culture Clash

The Clash continued to play with fellow London punk bands such as the Pistols and the Damned during the fall, including the failed *Anarchy Tour*. The Clash was soon signed to CBS Records, which released its first single, "White Riot," in March 1977, a call to arms for white Britons to rally around current social causes.

The band's vinyl debut came on April 8, 1977, with their self-titled release. It featured "White Riot," "Career Opportunities," "I'm So Bored with the U.S.A.," and a cover of the popular reggae song "Police and Thieves." The band's songs ranged from the simple and rollicking style of the Ramones to the rhythmic beats of Rastafarian music.

Jamaican reggae and ska had a profound influence on early punk rockers such as the Clash. Reggae's sound was unlike any other form of popular music, and it featured lyrics about endless political and social conflict that appealed to scene kids. Ska music added brass instruments to the rhythm section. The Clash incorporated reggae and ska into their music with great success.

The Clash was a hit in the United Kingdom, but it was not released in the United States for another two years. American record executives instead released the band's second album, *Give 'Em Enough Rope*, first. A more expensive overseas copy of *The Clash* sold more than one hundred thousand copies in America, making it the most successful import ever. Meanwhile, the Clash replaced drummer Chimes with Topper Headon.

The band's third release was the double album *London Calling* in December 1979. It was a major commercial and critical breakthrough and was

The Clash pioneered a unique sound by infusing their punk songs with elements of Jamaican reggae and ska.

arguably punk rock's highest achievement. *Rolling Stone* named it as number eight on its Top 500 Albums of All Time list in 2003. It featured the popular-worldwide singles "Train in Vain" and "Clampdown." But the most important single was the title track. Selected by *Rolling Stone* as the number fifteen song of all time, the uncharacteristic mid-tempo pace and chilling vocals of Strummer gave "London Calling" a haunting, apocalyptic sound.

The Death of Punk Rock

The Clash continued to triumph after the releases of the triple-album *Sandinista!* and *Combat Rock*, both of which sold well in the United Kingdom and the United States. The band had shied further away from its quick-beat punk rock roots and toward its own unique style. Hits from the two early 1980s albums included the piano-heavy dance beat "Rock the Casbah," the pre-hip-hop tune "The Magnificent Seven," and the reggae-heavy "Straight to Hell." Jones defended the band's departure from the early punk rock sound by saying: "There was a point where punk was going narrower and narrower, painting themselves into a corner. We thought we could just do any kind of music."[25]

Following the release of *Combat Rock*, Jones and Headon were both asked to leave the band. Strummer and Simonon attempted to revert back to

Standing between the Edge (far left) of the group U2 and an industry representative (far right), the surviving members of the Clash are inducted into the Rock and Roll Hall of Fame in 2003.

Buzzcocks

The pioneering British band Buzzcocks became the first punk rock band in the world to form their own independent record label. They called their label New Hormones. After New Hormones released its four-song debut *Spiral Scratch,* the group was signed to United Artists Records. Notable singles included "What Do I Get?" and "Ever Fallen in Love?" The group's lyrics were intelligent, alternating between tormented and humorous, and their songs were short and energetic. Their music laid the groundwork for what would later be called "pop punk."

The band had its origins in Manchester, England. Founding members Pete Shelley and Howard Devoto had met at college and were both fans of the Velvet Underground and Iggy Pop and the Stooges. In February 1976 they attended two Sex Pistols concerts in London and decided they wanted to start their own band. The name they picked was slang for "youngsters." At their first concert, in July 1976, they were the opening act for the Sex Pistols. Thanks in part to Buzzcock's popularity, Manchester became the second largest punk scene in England after London.

their early sound with the flop 1985 album *Cut the Crap*, which they both later disowned. The Clash officially broke up following that release. Most members of the band continued in music, with the exception of Headon, who battled his addiction to heroin. Strummer died of a heart attack on December 22, 2002, at the age of fifty. The Clash was inducted into the Rock and Roll Hall of Fame in March 2003.

Although the Clash continued to play well into the 1980s, most fans believed that punk rock had died out far earlier. After the Sex Pistols broke up in 1978, some considered the scene to be over. Still others claim that the death of Vicious in early 1979 marked the death of the punk rock era. Although it might seem like a short shelf life for such a popular form of music, its influences continued to live on.

Chapter Four

New Wave, Post-Punk, and Hardcore

W hile the Sex Pistols were still terrorizing conservative Britons and the Clash was touring in support of its debut, *The Clash*, the next direction of punk rock was beginning to form in America. In fact, punk rock would splinter into three major forms: New Wave, post-punk, and hardcore.

Riding the Wave

The term *New Wave* was originally just a pseudonym for punk rock. Many record companies and radio stations felt punk rock had been a fad, so it was given a new name in order to revive it. Eventually, New Wave bands shied away from the punk rock sound and began featuring mainstream pop songs and more commercial styles. Many other New Wave bands, including U2, R.E.M., and the Police, found massive commercial success as mainstream rock-and-roll groups, but they had little connection to the early punk rock scene.

One of the first New Wave bands was the Talking Heads. Previously, they had been considered punk, but with their fifth album, *Speaking in Tongues*, released in June 1983, the Heads broke through to major commercial success. They had their first hit single, "Burning Down the House," which made the American top-ten list and became a smash-hit music video.

Another CBGB alumni to find great success during the New Wave explosion was Blondie. Like their CBGB counterparts, it was Blondie's third album, *Parallel Lines*, released in September 1978, that brought the band fame. The record reached number one on the charts in the United Kingdom and featured the smash-hit singles "Heart of Glass," "One Way or Another," and "Hanging on the Telephone." The band followed up the success of *Parallel Lines* with *Eat to the Beat* in October 1979, which also reached the top of the charts in the United Kingdom. Blondie was also inducted into the Rock and Roll Hall of Fame in March 2006.

Like the punk rock scene that formed it, New Wave became known for some of its trademark fashions. Musicians and fans adored bright colors, spandex, and large earrings and bracelets. New Wave also involved the return of popular trends from the past such as thin neckties, pleats, and paisley prints. New Wave followers gained a renewed fascination of the Pop Art movement led by Warhol. Wild hairstyles became popular as well, such as overly wavy or poufed hair, made popular by the British New Wave band A Flock of Seagulls.

Punk After Punk

The second major genre created by the demise of punk rock was a predominantly British movement called post-punk. It was the middle ground between hardcore and New Wave. It lacked the furious pace of hardcore but had the same feelings of anger and confusion. It was not as pop oriented as New Wave but matched its experimental style. Early post-punk bands established the genre as commercially viable and thus created alternative rock by expanding the underground's sound into the fringes of mainstream rock.

One of the original post-punk bands was Public Image Ltd., formed by Lydon shortly after the Sex Pistols broke up in 1978. Public Image Ltd., or PIL, is recognized as the earliest post-punk band due to its complicated and unique sound that mixed reggae with progressive rock, noise, and sometimes even disco beats. Both of the band's early albums sold relatively well, but Lydon eventually dispersed the band in 1993 and released a solo album called *Psycho's Path* in 1997.

Another important member of the post-punk movement was the band the Cure. The Easy Cure, before the name was shortened, was originally formed by Robert Smith along with his schoolmates in 1976. Their early sound was lighter, though with an edgy tone. The Cure was credited with being one of

Mike Score of the New Wave band A Flock of Seagulls was known for his outrageous hairstyles.

the first goth rock bands due to their gloomy lyrics and lead singer Smith's ghoulish appearance. He wore heavy eye shadow, smudged red lipstick, and wildly messy black hair. The Cure's debut album, titled *Three Imaginary Boys*, was released in June 1979 to fair critical and commercial success.

The Cure continued with its solemn style into the 1980s with singles like "Close to Me" and "Why Can't I Be You?" The band began to find a popular audience in the 1990s when its ninth studio album, *Wish*, reached number one in the United Kingdom and number two in the United States. The Cure's influence can be seen on British alternative rock bands such as the Smiths and Radiohead, plus contemporary American goth bands such as AFI and Marilyn Manson.

A Hardcore Following

The third spawn of punk rock was called hardcore punk. The genre of hardcore punk is characterized by its intense tempo and context. Hardcore bands sped up the rhythm and beat of bands like the Ramones and the Sex Pistols to unheard-of speeds. Guitars screeched and drumbeats pounded to near-deafening levels during live performances. Like the Ramones' songs, hardcore songs were routinely shorter than any other type of music, usually around two minutes. Lyrics were often anarchistic and heavily critical of social values. Drugs and alcohol fueled the scene, and shows often became major melees in a matter of seconds. Byrne,

lead singer of the Talking Heads, said in the hardcore scene "you find punks who are really punks: mean as hell, and not just the creators of an interesting persona."[26]

As has been the case with every other form of underground and punk rock, hardcore came out of small social circles that sprang up independently across the United States. Important scenes existed in Los Angeles, San Francisco, and Washington, D.C. But hardcore never attained a large following outside of the small scenes and rarely received coverage from the press.

The Left Coast

Early hardcore scenes had a dedicated following in California. Los Angeles and Orange County were two neighboring communities that were very different from each other. Los Angeles was sprawling and ethnically diverse, while Orange County was relatively smaller and much more conservative. Both environments, however, would be prime for creating groups of disillusioned youth. Los Angeles had a large population, which aided the ability of youths to find others that they could relate to, and the conservative nature of Orange County led many kids there to rebel against authority.

One of the first and arguably most important Los Angeles hardcore bands was the group Black Flag. Guitarist Greg Ginn formed the band in 1976 under the original name Panic. A few years later the band changed its name to Black Flag, after the insecticide. The

Henry Rollins screeches into the microphone as Black Flag, arguably the most important L.A. hardcore band, performs in a 2003 reunion show.

name was also an implication of anarchy. Henry Rollins, a fan who lived in Washington, D.C., auditioned and became the lead singer in 1981, earning the band an instant notoriety. Rollins was muscular, tattooed, and extremely intense. During live performances he would constantly leave the stage to fight with the audience. His singing was fierce and full of passion, which gave the band the boost it needed. Black Flag released its first album, *Damaged*, later that year, which became an instant classic among fans.

Black Flag's true importance was not its sound, however. In fact, many experts have pointed out that despite being so renowned, the band's music style has never been considered influential. Instead, it was the band's work ethic and self-reliance that made it groundbreaking. The phrase "do it yourself," or DIY, became especially prominent during this time. Ginn had created his own record label called SST Records, which produced and released most of Black Flag's material. The band also achieved the first national tour by an independent band. By contacting owners and managers of small venues directly, the band was able to tour across the country several different times despite never being signed to a major record label.

The controversial band the Dead Kennedys was the driving force behind the hardcore scene in San Francisco.

Other important bands to surface out of Southern California included the Circle Jerks, fronted by Black Flag co-founder Keith Morris; the Germs, whose lead singer Darby Crash committed suicide in 1980; and TSOL, short for the True Sounds of Liberty.

San Francisco was also a major force in the hardcore scene. Unlike Southern California, where the authorities constantly policed shows, the Bay-area hardcore scene was aided by the city's liberal attitude. The most successful band to emerge from San Francisco was the Dead Kennedys. Lead singer and songwriter Jello Biafra fronted the Kennedys, who were always controversial and known for their biting sense of humor. Biafra's lyrics were staunchly left-wing and openly critical of President Ronald Reagan and other conservative aspects of society. Biafra himself ran for mayor of San Francisco in 1979 with a political platform of disallowing cars in the city, forcing businesspeople to wear clown suits to work, and allowing squatting in abandoned buildings. He finished in the fourth position out of ten candidates. As with the Sex Pistols, workers refused to handle Dead Kennedys albums due to their offensive band name, which referred to the assassinated politicians and brothers John Kennedy and Robert Kennedy.

The Dead Kennedys were also similar to Black Flag in terms of their importance to the hardcore scene. Like Ginn, Biafra founded his own record company, Alternative Tentacles, which released all of their studio albums. The Kennedys also failed to earn much commercial success in the United States and United Kingdom and were not stylistically influential to future bands. But like Black Flag, their DIY mind-set became a significant model for making underground music more accessible and for helping spread it across America.

The East Coast

Along the East Coast of the United States, limited hardcore scenes existed in New York City, Boston, New Jersey, and most notably, Washington, D.C. Like the California scenes, the East Coast bands had very small but dedicated followings. One of the earliest bands was the New Jersey outfit the Misfits, formed in 1977. They took their name from Marilyn Monroe's final film. Being big fans of old science fiction, horror, and B-movies, the band incorporated aspects of these into their records and live shows. Lead singer Glenn Danzig's sinister lyrics, harsh attitude, and love for the mystical earned him the nickname "Evil Elvis." The Misfits were credited with creating the subgenre horror punk, and many of the more morbid contemporary punk rock bands cite them as a major influence.

The most important hardcore DIY acts hailed from the nation's capital. The first of these bands was the all-black Bad Brains. They had originally formed as a jazz band but found groups like the Sex Pistols and Black Sabbath more interesting. The fact that all four

Moshing and Crowd Surfing

The hardcore scene in California was at times a very violent setting. Fans had taken the pogo dance, which was non-violent hopping, that the Pistols had created and turned it into the dangerous slam dance. The slam dance, or moshing, involved shoving, swinging arms, and throwing elbows. Oftentimes, slam dancing would lead to fistfights breaking out among crowd members. The mosh pit, or pit circle, is a circular hollow in the middle of the crowd where participants run, hop, and dance in a circle while slamming into each other. Moshing is still found at contemporary punk rock shows, though many venues have "no moshing" policies or place security guards to maintain safety.

Jello Biafra also created the act of stage diving, in which a band member or a fan who gets access to the stage jumps down onto the crowd during the show. Stage diving in turn created crowd surfing, which involves audience members being "floated" across the crowd by fans holding them up. Rowdy Los Angeles crowds led to many Southern California venues barring hardcore bands from performing due to the damage caused by their fans.

Fans of hardcore slam dance in a mosh pit during a 2004 show in Chicago.

members of Washington's earliest hardcore influence were African American was interesting, given that members of the punk rock scene have always been predominantly white. Formed in 1977, Bad Brains have been considered the founders of hardcore punk due to the fervent pace of many of their songs. On the other hand, they mixed reggae and funk into their music as well, although they kept their punk songs separate from their reggae songs.

Bad Brains earned a reputation for having unruly live performances. Their lead singer, H.R., would jump wildly around the stage and into the crowd. As a result, the band received an unofficial ban from the few Washington clubs. Eventually they relocated to New York City and wrote the song "Banned in D.C." about their experience. In December 1981 the New York–based ROIR Records released Bad Brains' self-titled debut on cassette tape.

Another DIY punk band from Washington formed in 1980 and called themselves Minor Threat. Founders Ian MacKaye and Jeff Nelson were both in an earlier hardcore band called the Teen Idles. After they broke up, MacKaye and Nelson formed Minor Threat along with two other classmates from prep school. The band played its first live show in December 1980. Minor Threat is considered the epitome of hardcore punk; the band combined cynical songs about politics and society with the fast tempo and DIY ethic of the hardcore scene.

Although Minor Threat recorded only a few dozen songs, their real strength was in their live performances. Lead singer MacKaye was immensely

Regarded by many as the fathers of hardcore punk, Bad Brains played their own brand of reggae and funk and also punk music to create a unique sound.

charismatic, and his disgust with society seemed to fuel his rage. He seethed about the establishment, corruption, and the apathy of youth toward important political issues. His energy transferred to the crowd, who screamed his words back at him. He would even pass the microphone around to audience members so that everyone would become part of the show. Minor Threat broke up in 1983 in part because MacKaye felt there were too many other bands doing the same thing.

David Johansen, front man of the New York Dolls, holds up a copy of the popular fanzine beetle *featuring a picture of him on the cover.*

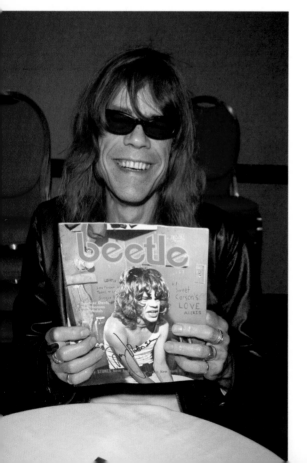

After Minor Threat parted ways, a fan named Guy Picciotto was inspired to create his own band named Rites of Spring. The name came from the famously divisive classical ballet by Igor Stravinsky, and Picciotto's band proved to be as groundbreaking as its namesake. The band still maintained the guttural singing, heavy guitars, and quick drumbeats of earlier hardcore bands but sang about emotions and sentiments that were unknown to the scene. Rites slowly built a small following through word of mouth. Although they only played sixteen shows in two years, their performances became a phenomenon. Fans of hardcore had matured and grown weary of being outcasts, and at shows audience members would openly weep at the emotion on display. Rites and their growing fan base became jokingly referred to as emotional hardcore, or emocore for short.

Fanzine Phenomenon

Common to every hardcore scene across America, the DIY ethic was what made hardcore punk a unique scene; despite their small numbers, the punk rockers had always found a way to connect with one another and keep informed about the latest happenings. One way they were successful in achieving this was the creation of scenes and hangout spots where they could all mingle. Another method of staying connected was through homemade magazines called fanzines.

Fanzines were the work of dedicated fans and were vastly different from mainstream music publications such as *Rolling Stone* and *Creem*. For one thing, fanzines were usually only available through mailing lists or at shows. While commercial magazines featured full-color, glossy pages, paid writers and contributors, and professional teams to design layouts, fanzines were black-and-white with crude layouts and no page numbers, and they were often photocopied and stapled together. The illustrations, photographs, comic strips, and collages were all of amateur quality. Fanzines were cheap to buy and generated no revenue.

In terms of content, major fanzines with a circulation greater than one thousand copies touched on music, politics, art, and sometimes more obscure topics. Musically, they featured interviews with artists, album reviews, and news about upcoming shows. They had political commentaries and editorials, which were usually liberal or anarchistic.

The most influential initial fanzines were *Punk* from New York City and *Sniffin' Glue* from London. Both were formed during the early stages of punk rock and were important in spreading news through the growing scenes. Their examples led to thousands of other fanzines springing up across America during the hardcore movement. The Los Angeles scene had two popular fanzines, *Slash* and *Flipside*. The former was more intellectual, while the latter was described as "straight-forward, dumb fun."[27] A more radical fanzine is Minneapolis's *Profane Existence*, which dealt mostly with anarchist politics and political bands.

The most influential fanzine from the hardcore punk era was *Maximum Rock N Roll* from San Francisco. It was started in 1982 as an extension of a punk radio show of the same name and was able to go into more depth politically than the radio show. It started out as a local fanzine but expanded to include scene reports from every state in the United States as well as international coverage, and it remains an influential source for contemporary punk rockers. The staff is all volunteers and the fanzine is nonprofit. The organization has also established Pressure Drop Press, which has published anarchistic works; the Epicenter, a cheap record store and fanzine library; and the Gilman Street Project, an all-ages venue that supports punk rock.

Financial Independence

A further aspect of the DIY ethic was the establishment of independent record labels by the artists themselves. In the past, punk rock bands relied on major labels to sign them and release their records. This became a problem after bands such as the Sex Pistols, the Clash, and the Velvet Underground ran into trouble with their conservative record labels. Author Charles O'Hara explains the hardcore scene's recognition of the dilemma:

> Many of the original Punk bands of the mid-70's were later signed and exploited by major labels. It

Music Television

MTV—Music Television—began to broadcast music videos starting at midnight on August 1, 1981. The first video aired was, ironically, *Video Killed the Radio Star* by the Buggles. As the channel grew in popularity, record companies began to market their bands with music videos in order to boost record sales. In MTV's initial years, mainstays included the funky Michael Jackson, the controversial diva Madonna, and the New Wave reincarnation of David Bowie.

Music videos and MTV became a major influence on popular culture. Video jockeys introduced new fashion trends and slang terms. MTV was also the only television channel fully dedicated to around-the-clock music programming until the formation of its sister station, VH-1—Video Hits 1—in 1985. MTV also helped to popularize new genres, including hip-hop and heavy metal.

MTV also had a profound effect on many New Wave bands. Since MTV had a relatively small budget to work with and nonstop airtime to fill, they acquired the rights to many New Wave bands for little money. The Talking Heads and Blondie received constant airplay for singles such as "Burning Down the House" and "Rapture," respectively. Consequently, music videos resulted in major publicity for New Wave bands and helped them achieve massive sales.

took the first wave of British anarchists and California Punks to realize that they could do records on their own. This way they could set their own prices, write their own lyrics and play the music that they felt was important with no threat of compromise.[28]

Ginn of Black Flag and Biafra of the Dead Kennedys both started their own modest record labels to release their own music. MacKaye and Nelson of Minor Threat also formed their own record label in 1980 called Dischord Records, which released all of their material along with that of Rites of Spring. Dischord produced, distributed, and sold all their releases via catalog and completely independent from major record labels.

Musicians began to recognize the freedom that independence from major record labels brought, and they took advantage. Brett Gurewitz from the Los Angeles hardcore band Bad Religion formed one of the most successful independent labels, called Epitaph Records, in the early 1980s. Originally, Epitaph was a small label that released Bad Religion's early releases. Throughout the rest of the decade and into the 1990s, Epitaph began to snatch up groups that would soon hit it big when pop punk boomed in the mid-1990s. One of these groups was the Orange County–based band the Offspring, whose third album, *Smash*, sold 11 million copies worldwide in 1994 and became the best-selling independent release of all time. The Offspring's lead singer, Dexter Holland, then created his own label a year later called Nitro Records.

It was the creation of independent labels that allowed for the proliferation of pop-punk and skate-punk bands to seek radio airplay and commercial success in the 1990s. And as major successes, punk rock bands saw their greatest influences on popular culture yet.

Chapter Five

Punk Becomes Popular

The splintering of the punk rock genre continued past the New Wave, post-punk, and hardcore punk movements of the 1980s and went straight through to the 1990s. The difference this time was that the new forms of punk rock finally broke into mainstream commercial success with stunningly unexpected results.

Punk rock was known for its limited underground following, anticorporate themes, quick tempos, and angst-filled content. This formula was repeated throughout the country in various scenes and led to local success. Major movements appeared in Southern California, San Francisco, and Washington, D.C. There was also a small scene in the Pacific Northwest, most notably in Seattle, where shows were poorly attended and the audience was usually only made up of members of other bands. Notable Seattle bands such as Mudhoney, Green River, and the Melvins were early examples of the new genre called grunge.

Grunge Reaches Perfection

Mark Arm, future lead singer of Green River and Mudhoney, originally coined the term *grunge* in 1981 when he was describing his band to a Seattle fanzine. He said the band had a dirty sound from the heavy guitar distortion that grunge bands utilized. A local independent record label used the term several years later to publicize Green River. As the Seattle sound grew in popularity, the term *grunge* became a media buzzword and was used around the world in reference to this type of music. Despite this new term, the Seattle scene of the 1980s and early 1990s was in actual fact punk rock.

The most famous of the grunge bands was Nirvana. When the band hit it big in 1991, it essentially became the most popular and successful punk rock band ever. Nirvana's importance to punk rock and even rock and roll has been highly publicized: "Without [Elvis] Presley, rock and roll itself might never have got off the ground.

Mark Arm, the lead singer of Mudhoney, coined the term grunge in 1981 during an interview with a Seattle fanzine.

Without the Beatles, it could have faded away. Without the [Sex] Pistols, it would have grown old and fat. And without Nirvana, commercial rock would still be where it was at the beginning of the 1990's, with nothing exciting happening at all."[29] Childhood friends Kurt Cobain and Krist Novoselic formed the band in 1987 in Aberdeen, Washington. After featuring several different drummers, Nirvana finally recruited Dave Grohl in 1991.

Cobain was the band's lead singer, guitarist, and major songwriter. He wrote songs about depression and frustration. His voice was piercing and unique, described as "a painful yell that started somewhere around his stomach then spent the rest of the song looking for a way out."[30] The band's first major single was "Smells Like Teen Spirit," which hit number one on charts around the world. The music video for the song was also a huge hit on MTV and is revered as one of the best videos ever. In it, the band performs in a dim high school gymnasium and quickly turns a pep rally into a mosh pit.

The single was from Nirvana's second full-length album, *Nevermind*, released in September 1991. The title came from Cobain's love for the Sex Pistols and his respect for their album, *Never Mind the Bollocks*. Nirvana became an instant sensation upon the release of *Nevermind*. Despite being

Kurt Cobain was the lead singer of the band Nirvana, one of the most influential pioneers of the alternative sound of grunge music.

around since 1987 and having a moderate following in Seattle, no one, especially not the band's label Geffen Records, expected the blockbuster success of *Nevermind*. It sold 3 million copies in its first six months, reaching triple-platinum status, and became the top-selling album in America. It was the first punk rock record to reach number one on the American record charts. It also featured other smash-hit top-ten singles "Come As You Are," "Lithium," and "In Bloom."

The band members were never comfortable with the popularity they earned. This became a recurring theme with other Seattle grunge bands, such as Pearl Jam, that sold nearly as well as Nirvana. Cobain was determined to give the band's next album an edgier sound to counteract Nirvana's commercial success, and he sought out punk rock producer Steve Albini. Their creation was Nirvana's third studio album, *In Utero*, released in September 1993, which also reached number one on album charts around the world. Two months after the release of *In Utero*, the band performed an acoustic set for MTV's *Unplugged*, which became another chart topper and won a Grammy for best alternative music album after its release in November 1994.

Despite being universally acclaimed, the album was haunting due to the recent fate of Cobain. On April 8, 1994, an electrician discovered Cobain's lifeless body in a small room above Cobain's garage. Fueled by an ongoing heroin addiction and a battle with depression, Cobain committed suicide by shooting himself in the head with a shotgun. He was only twenty-seven, and the news of his suicide shocked the public and especially the music industry. His death has since become a major landmark in the history of rock and roll, due to Nirvana's groundbreaking success as the creators of mainstream alternative rock.

The numerous fans of Nirvana began to seek out new bands after Nirvana's demise. They had gotten a taste of the raw and sometimes threatening sound of the underground. Author Andy Greenwald explained the post-grunge phenomenon in his book, *Nothing Feels Good:*

> Like it or not, subculture was now big business and regional and independent acts gained access to the national stage. There was no such thing as national punk until Nirvana. . . . A generation of high schoolers suddenly declared themselves fans of independent music; being punk was mainstream. Those who felt their heads spin around upon first listen to *Nevermind* went out in search of new fixes.[31]

Journey to the End of East Bay

It was in the small California city of Berkeley that a more mainstream breed of hardcore was forming that would take over the direction of punk rock.

Grunge had begun to die out after Cobain's death and the other popular grunge bands' refusal to begin catering to the mainstream sound. A small music club called Gilman was where the most important Berkeley punk rock bands got their start.

One of the earliest bands to emerge from Gilman was the ska-punk band Operation Ivy, also called Op Ivy. The group formed in May 1987 and included guitarist and vocalist Tim Armstrong and bassist Matt Freeman. True to the DIY ethic, the band was only together for two years but played an incredible 185 live shows while also recording two releases, the EP—which is longer than a single but shorther than an album—*Hectic* and the full-length *Energy*. The band later re-released *Energy* to include tracks from *Hectic* and from a compilation for Lookout! Records. After Op Ivy broke up in May 1989, Freeman and Armstrong created a new band called Rancid.

Armstrong and Freeman enlisted drummer Brett Reed and later singer and guitarist Lars Frederiksen. They recorded their first demo with Lookout! Records and were signed to the independent label Epitaph, run by Bad Religion's Gurewitz. Their 1995 release . . . *And Out Come the Wolves* featured MTV and radio hits "Ruby Soho," "Time Bomb," and "Roots Radicals." The image of a lonely punk on the album cover was a tribute to Minor Threat's self-titled album sleeve, and the title was in reference to the furious attempts by major record labels to sign Rancid. Despite the interest, the band remained independent and retained its creative control by staying with Epitaph.

The band's diverse style has become its trademark. As Op Ivy, Armstrong and Freeman had mixed vigorous punk rock with ska. As Rancid, songs varied from fast-paced hardcore to slower ska and reggae jams. Rancid mixed great talent with amateurishness.

Previously, punk rock had flourished because of the perception that anyone could form his or her own band, but this perception started to change in the early 1990s. For example, bassist Freeman was one of punk rock's first great bass strummers. Rather than use the bass to help establish the rhythm of its songs, Rancid often used Freeman's skill to play the melody, usually the guitarist's job. Examples can be found in the remarkable bass solos in the first track of . . . *And Out Come the Wolves*, "Maxwell Murder," and in "Journey to the End of the East Bay," a song that chronicles the Op Ivy story. The opposite of Freeman's talent were Armstrong and Frederikson's muttering vocal styles. Their method of exaggerated singing at times leaves them indecipherable and out of tune.

The King of Pop Punk

The most successful Berkeley band was the pop-punk trio Green Day. Like Op Ivy and Rancid, Green Day also started off its career by performing often at Gilman. The band consisted of Billie Joe Armstrong on vocals and guitar, Mike Dirnt on bass, and Tré

The band Rancid earned a loyal following with its own style of music that balanced fast-paced hardcore songs with slower ska and reggae jams.

Cool on the drums. After the death of Cobain, Green Day took over the punk rock reins and became the biggest crossover success punk rock has ever seen. In stark contrast to Nirvana's dark and edgy sound, Green Day offered upbeat punk rock with a more light-hearted approach to teenage confusion.

Green Day's major label debut was the sensational album *Dookie*, released in February 1994. Led by five hugely popular singles, including three number one hits, "Longview," "Basket-case," and "When I Come Around,"

Dookie sold 10 million copies. The band also made memorable videos for their singles that received constant airplay on MTV. Green Day then embarked on a major national and international tour, which included an infamous mud fight with fans at Woodstock 1994, and also won a Grammy for best alternative music performance.

The sound featured on *Dookie* was much lighter than previous punk rock bands, such as Green Day's idols the Sex Pistols and the Clash. The band did not dabble in politics or even

924 Gilman

Berkeley, California, is a college town across the bay from downtown San Francisco and north of the blue-collar city of Oakland. It is well-known for its liberal and sometimes eccentric residents and the original University of California campus. The street culture is very open and is home to many transients, pervasive drug use, and a love of the liberal arts. It is also home of the influential fanzine *Maximum Rock N Roll*, which uses volunteer-run and nonprofit organizations to spread punk rock and preserve its history.

One of these establishments is the Gilman Street Project, located at 924 Gilman Street in North Berkeley. The Gilman was founded in 1986 as an all-ages venue that sought to create a drug-, alcohol-, and violence-free environment. The bands that perform there are predominantly punk rock bands that cannot be sexist, racist, or signed to a major label. Admission to the shows is very inexpensive, and newcomers are charged a unique one-time membership fee. *Maximum Rock N Roll* explains the policy: "Anyone can join for a mere $2 and a commitment to participate in a violence-free, vandalism-free environment."

Quoted in Craig O'Hara, *The Philosophy of Punk*. San Francisco, CA: AK Press, 1999, p. 164.

complicated emotions. Songs were about masturbation and casual drug use, yet their catchy melodies and sing-along choruses managed to deflect much of the controversy. Rock journalist Jim DeRogatis wrote in an article for *BAM* magazine:

More important than selling records and making a racket, Green Day is teaching a new and very young audience that punk is about four things: doing away with rock-star posing, supporting a do-it-yourself ideal, turning just about everything into a joke, and playing catchy, hard-hitting rock 'n' roll in the style of Chuck Berry at the tempo of the Ramones.[32]

Green Day's next album was the slightly darker *Insomniac*, released in October 1995. The album was considered a disappointment compared to the band's previous record, but it still sold over 2 million copies, which was a major feat for a punk rock band. By now, Green Day had become cemented in the alternative rock scene, which had grown into a major genre due in part to the success of Nirvana, Pearl Jam, and *Dookie*. Green Day had even been denied the right to play at Gilman because they were now considered to be too commercial.

Green Day productively continued its career into the first decade of the 2000s with a maturing and expanding musical palette. In the 1990s it had proven that punk rock could be commercially popular, and many other pop-punk bands soon followed.

A *Smash* Hit

The Offspring was another band that toiled in the underground scene for many years before achieving mainstream success. The band formed in Orange County in 1984, but a decade later its third album, *Smash*, put the Offspring's name in lights. The band had recorded its self-titled debut in 1989 with the hardcore sound, morbid lyrics, and liberal politics of early influences like the Damned and the Germs. Epitaph Records had heard the Offspring's early recordings and decided to produce the band's follow-up releases. First came *Ignition* in March 1993, then *Smash* in August 1994.

The Offspring's sound had gradually begun to change its style away from the underground punk of the band's first album to the mixture of pop punk and heavy metal heard in *Smash*. The album was an instant success and outsold Nirvana's *Nevermind* and Green Day's *Dookie*. With 11 million records sold and a diamond record certification, the Epitaph-released *Smash* became the best-selling independent-label record of all time. It featured instantly recognizable teenage anthems such as "Self Esteem" and "Come Out and Play (Keep 'Em Separated)." The album cover was also striking, with its X-ray negative of a human skull and ribcage. It was also the only time the band dropped the article *the* from their name.

After the success of *Smash*, the Offspring left Epitaph and signed with the major label Columbia Records. The band once again achieved a major hit in November 1998 with *Americana*. It was the Offspring's fifth album and marked the band's departure from punk rock toward mainstream alternative rock. This is most evident in the silly singles "Pretty Fly (for a White Guy)" and "Why Don't You Get a Job?" The standout track was the single "The Kids Aren't Alright," which had a pessimistic title and message in sharp contrast to the 1965 feel-good song by The Who named "The Kids Are Alright."

Don't blink Now

As yet another California pop-punk band in the tradition of Green Day, the Offspring, and Rancid, San Diego's blink-182 broke into record charts with music more sugary and lyrics more immature than any of its predecessors. The trio had released a few demos and EPs plus a full-length debut album before it began to turn heads in the late 1990s. The band's first album with the major label MCA Records was *Dude Ranch*, released in June 1997. The album contained a perfect example of pop punk in the form of the anthemic "Damnit," a song about breaking up driven by repetitive guitar riffs and constant snare drums.

The main contributions of blink-182 to pop punk came with *Enema of the State* and *Take Off Your Pants and Jacket*, two chart-topping albums with lyrical content as juvenile and crude as their titles suggest. Guitarist and vocalist Tom Delonge explains the band's shallow content and toilet humor: "Everyone always asks us if we have a philosophy, what our band is supposed to mean. We're just trying to have a good time, trying to make ourselves laugh, and make the kids laugh. We don't have a bigger message than that."[33] The band also brought a new demographic to the genre of punk rock. The recent popularity of pop punk made the youth-based movements of previous decades seem like centuries ago. The anti-commercial mindset of 1970s punk rock had given way to industry corporatization in the 1990s. This new type of punk rock was now all over youth-oriented television networks, and blink-182 and its counterparts such as New Found Glory, Good Charlotte, and Simple Plan dominated MTV, followed by a bastion of mostly teenage girls.

The Rise of Emo

The small subgenre of hardcore punk called emocore, or emotional hardcore, had been quiet for a number of years until the early 1990s bands Jawbreaker and Sunny Day Real Estate released groundbreaking albums that brought emocore to the public's notice. Author Andy Greenwald explains the appeal of emocore: "Frustrated hardcore kids began to see emo[core] as a way to marry the intensity they found so appealing with the surprising and discomforting range of emotions brought on by growing older."[34]

Since emocore bands played to the same tempos and belonged to the same scenes as hardcore bands, many fans found that it was an effective way of easing out of the hardcore scene and into the more genuine and constructive emocore style. While grunge was in its prime and pop punk was waiting next in line, emocore was developing a more challenging sound that would eventually take over.

When It Pains It Roars

The three members of the band Jawbreaker met while attending New York University (NYU) together in 1986. Upon graduating, the trio moved to San Francisco, where it became a part of the local music scene, including making several appearances at Gilman. The band released its second album, *Bivouac*, in October 1992 and its third album, *24 Hour Revenge Therapy*, in March 1994 on small, independent labels.

By then Jawbreaker had developed a dedicated fan base via its local shows and national tours. Blake Schwartzenbach, the lead singer, guitarist, and major songwriter, had become a cult hero among the scene kids. His songs were heartfelt and dealt with relatable issues.

For example, songs on *24 Hour Revenge Therapy* took place in the moments immediately following the end of a relationship. Schwartzenbach had earned degrees in English and creative writing from NYU, and his lyrics reflected his skill with words. His lyrics ranged from metaphorical and obscure to straightforward and heart wrenching and were always the differentiating factor between Jawbreaker and other bands of the time.

Starting in October 1993, however, the band began to alienate their devoted following. They played several live shows with Nirvana in the Midwest, which fans perceived as selling out. Despite being strongly against corporate record labels and the big-business music industry, Jawbreaker signed with Geffen Records in late 1994, further alienating fans who continued to see the band as hypocritical. Even so, the band recorded *Dear You* with Green Day producer Rob Cavallo, which was released in 1995. Again, former fans criticized the band, this time because Schwartzenbach's trademark raspy voice had been smoothed out and the band's amateur recording aesthetic was gone.

Seen here in concert in 2002, blink-182 popularized punk music among a largely affluent middle-class demographic.

Untitled and Grown-Up

As the prototypical immature pop-punk band of the late 1990s, blink-182 released songs that varied from fantasizing about Princess Leia from Star Wars to wearing disposable diapers. Previous music videos featured the band running naked through city streets and parodying popular boy-band clichés. The band had made its name by being silly, and this made its matured 2003 release a risky move.

Often incorrectly considered a self-titled or ironically titled album, *(Untitled)* showed a side of the band that few had seen before. Now older, married, and parents, the band members loaded *(Untitled)* with surprising sentiment and unmistakable talent. The sound is less generic, an escape from pop punk into the introverted and experimental world of post-punk. Gone are the jokes and simple hooks of previous radio hits, replaced with singles such as the touching "I Miss You" and the regret-filled "Down." The most memorable songs come near the end, with the Cure front man Robert Smith singing on the lingering "All of This" and the impressive drum solo by Travis Barker in "I'm Lost Without You" in the record's final seconds.

From the band's early days of producing childish lyrics, blink-182 matured in later years to write more memorable songs.

Emerging from Seattle's grunge scene, Sunny Day Real Estate became the founders of a new genre of music known as emo.

A Ray of Sunshine

In contrast to Jawbreaker, the other landmark emocore band of the early 1990s was notably more hopeful. Coming out of the grunge scene of the Pacific Northwest, Sunny Day Real Estate was signed to the same label that had released Nirvana's first album, *Bleach*. Record executives were eager to find the successor to grunge, and in 1993 Sunny Day's front man, Jeremy Enigk, impressed Seattle's Sub Pop Records.

Released in 1994, Sunny Day's debut album, *Diary*, was the breakthrough that kick-started the emo movement and the achievement that proved that emo could become a commercial success. Songs featured quiet and thoughtful moments, and Enigk actually sang, rather than screaming or grinding out the most important parts of each song. After dispersing, Sunny Day released *LP2*, which included songs from unused material of the past. At the turn of the century, the band reunited and released two more albums.

Sunny Day Real Estate's initial success with *Diary* had paved the way for more emocore (now commonly referred to as emo) bands to find success in the second half of the 1990s. Most

Skate Punk

Skateboarding began much like punk rock did: as an extreme underground movement among teenagers in the 1970s. The connection between punk rock and skateboarding began with Southern California hardcore bands such as Black Flag and the Circle Jerks. Skateboarding publications such as *Thrasher* often featured hardcore and pop-punk bands in their magazines and played their music in videos showcasing extreme stunts. Many casual and professional skateboarders started their own bands in the 1980s and 1990s, such as Duane Peters's band, U.S. Bombs. As hardcore punk died out, a new genre called skate punk saw limited success in the early 1990s.

The most popular skate-punk bands were the Los Angeles–based Bad Religion, NOFX, and Pennywise. All three bands were similar in content; they were anarchistic and deeply pessimistic about society and popular culture, and they played fast-paced songs led by frantic drumbeats. Each scored a handful of successful radio hits but never major commercial success. Skate punk also made skate brand t-shirts and punk rock band T-shirts, hats worn unconventionally, and flat-soled heavy-duty skate shoes all popular. It also led to the term *poseurs*, which is branded on someone who is deemed to dress as a skater without actually being one.

of these bands were from the Midwest and Southwest, and not coincidentally. Like hardcore in conservative Orange County in the early 1980s, emo scenes were the most productive in so-called boring towns where kids turned to music to escape mundane living. Popular bands included the Get Up Kids from Kansas, Braid from Illinois, the Promise Ring from Wisconsin, and Jimmy Eat World from Arizona. Heading into the twenty-first century, emo would take over as the predominant style of punk rock.

Chapter Six

Punks of the Twenty-first Century

T he new forms of punk rock continued to be major contributors in mainstream music and popular culture forums well into the first decade of the new millennium. New technologies have led to an influx of successful bands, local scenes, and independent record labels by making the spreading of music much easier.

Fast and affordable personal computers and software have made recording and mixing studio-quality music possible at home or in small studios. The introduction of compressed computer audio files such as MP3s has resulted in a boom in their purchase and trade. The growth in popularity of MP3s led to the marketing of inexpensive MP3 players such as the iPod, which became as much of a fashion statement as it was a practical music player. This all created a large demand for, and easy access to, new music.

The Internet has had the biggest effect on independent music. On their Web sites, bands are able to offer se- lections of their music, show off music videos, announce upcoming tour dates, sell merchandise, and provide online forums for fans to communicate with band members and each other. Online retailers offer an infinitely larger selection than record stores, shipping even hard-to-find music to anywhere in the world. The Internet also allows independent record labels to reach larger audiences and are no longer limited to selling records only in local stores. Chat rooms build buzz for upcoming bands, and users illegally swap music files with each other. Discovering new bands no longer requires going to shows or purchasing albums; they are just a click away.

Redefining Genres

The expansion of independent music has created even more specific categories for punk rock. The most common categories are hardcore, emocore, the broad new genre called emo, and pop punk. Bands such as New Found

Pop artist Avril Lavigne holds up a plaque celebrating the platinum status of her 2002 debut album Let Go.

Glory, Simple Plan, and Good Charlotte have become the most prevalent pop-punk bands. Newcomers include Chicago's Fall Out Boy and Canada's Avril Lavigne and Sum 41.

Lavigne's arrival marked a particular change in pop punk. The most well-known pop-punk bands had been making plenty of watered-down punk rock with no real message—songs designed specifically for the airwaves. But Lavigne's June 2002 debut album, *Let Go*, which sold over 15 million copies worldwide, exposed pop punk for what it had become: a popular trend. Longtime punk rock fans and artists fiercely criticized her music and labeled Lavigne as Britney Spears in punk rock clothing. Pop punk had roped in hoards of adolescents who could identify with the ever-increasing level of teenage-relationship anxiety contained in its lyrics. This caused a major backlash from so-called old-school fans, who understood that punk rock had always been the opposition to popular culture. Resentment has been particularly pointed toward pop-punk-scene kids by fans of twenty-first-century hardcore.

The most popular hardcore bands of the new century were actually a mixture of earlier incarnations of punk rock genres like hardcore and skate punk plus early heavy metal. Bands like the Bled, As I Lay Dying, and Against Me! typically mix the fervent drumming style of skate punk with the driving guitars of heavy metal and the passionate singing of 1980s hardcore punk.

Another band that got its start at Gilman in Berkeley was the gothic hardcore band AFI. Short for A Fire Inside, AFI was signed to Offspring front man Holland's Nitro Records and developed a dedicated fan base through releases like *AFI* and *The Art of Drowning*. Like the Offspring and fellow San Francisco Bay–area band Green Day, the band was accused of selling out when it signed with the major label DreamWorks and released *Sing the Sorrow* in March 2003. AFI may have lost some of its most devoted fans, but it gained new ones when the album peaked at number five on the *Billboard* charts.

Another spin-off from punk rock is the updated form of emocore, also sometimes called post-hardcore or screamo. The original emocore created by Rites of Spring and furthered by Jawbreaker was not as layered and complex as the newer version. Although Sunny Day Real Estate's sound was closer to modern emocore than its predecessors, it still fell short of the style made popular by the most successful of the new emocore bands. The most common aspects in emocore now are dueling guitars and interweaving vocals. Bands such as Taking Back Sunday, Thrice, and the Used create a wall of chaotic sound that is surprisingly melodic at the same time.

Emovement

The largest new genre, and the most diverse and artistic, was the new emo category. It had matured and

Napster

The controversial computer program called Napster sparked the MP3 phenomenon that forever changed the face of the music industry. Developed by Shawn Fanning, it became popular in late 1999 when it offered users a nearly endless supply of free music downloads. The program was based on peer-to-peer sharing, which allowed users to access files directly from another person's computer. This created fast downloads and made even hard-to-find songs easy to locate. As millions of people began using it daily, problems quickly began to surface. One problem was Napster's popularity among college students, which resulted in the overloading and crashing of network servers across the country. The more predominant problem was the widespread piracy that led to the intervention of the federal government on behalf of the music industry. The program was shut down, and future downloaders were threatened with fines and jail time for infringing upon copyrighted material. Napster was relaunched a few years later as a paid subscription service.

Napster founder Shawn Fanning almost single-handedly launched the MP3 phenomenon that dramatically altered the music industry.

advanced along the same lines as emocore during the 1980s and 1990s. The earnest lyrics of Jawbreaker and the poignant melodies of Sunny Day inspired new fans who were liberated by the bands' unique emotional content. Pioneering new bands not only sold well, they also inspired countless others. The emo movement created a domino effect.

One of the earliest and most influential emo bands was Jimmy Eat World from Phoenix, Arizona. After signing with Capitol Records, Jimmy Eat World recorded *Static Prevails*, which became the first emocore record released by a major label in June 1996. The sound of that album was typical of the emocore being played by most bands of the time, alternating between loud bouts of screaming and quiet, thoughtful moments. After releasing its next album, *Clarity*, with Capitol, Jimmy Eat World was dropped by the label. The band next signed with DreamWorks, which released its hit album *Bleed American* in July 2001. After the terrorist attacks on September 11, 2001, the record was renamed *Jimmy Eat World* to avoid controversy. The self-titled release became one of the first successful emo albums in mainstream rock, fueled by the radio hit "The Middle."

Guitarist Jim Adkins of the wildly popular emo band Jimmy Eat World performs a solo during a 2005 concert.

By the time of *Jimmy Eat World*'s release, the definition of emocore had changed. Emocore had realigned with more hardcore bands. It seemed that the original emocore bands of the mid-1990s that survived long enough were stripped of their genre. The changeover began most notably in 1998 when Wisconsin's the Promise Ring was labeled as emo and a band to watch in the upcoming year by *Teen People* magazine. This created the vague category that has become even vaster than any other punk rock subgenre yet. Emo has been described as a "soundtrack to youth,"[35] more of a subculture than just a type of music. *Emo* also strangely became a derogatory term. Kids had no problem taking part in scenes and attending shows, but being branded "emo" was more of an accusation than a description, lumping kids together and stereotyping them as nerdy, overly sensitive, effeminate, and melodramatic.

The one thing that all emo bands have in common is their personal content matter. Songs are most often about friendship, love, heartbreak, losing loved ones, and feeling left out or depressed. In short, emo bands concentrate on eliciting certain emotional reactions from their lyrics. Even this guideline is vague, however. Bands can range from hopelessly heartfelt, like Dashboard Confessional, to morbid, like Alkaline Trio, and spiteful, like Saves the Day. Another similarity is that nearly all emo bands form strong connections with their fans. Just as British punk rock helped Londoners vent their frustration, emo helps fans find therapy through their music.

In many ways punk rock and emo are polar opposites. Early punk rock was about the destruction of the complex style of progressive rock, while emo is a celebration of musical talent. Founders of the punk rock movement like Johnny Rotten despised rock stars and sought the demystification of rock, whereas front men such as Dashboard Confessional's Chris Carrabba and My Chemical Romance's Gerard Way have become emo idols. Finally, while emo kids tend to be liberal, they are generally not anarchistic or rebellious in the same way that their punk rock precursors were.

However, there are some things that early punk rock and emo have in common. Although some front men are largely idolized, most emo musicians are unassuming and accessible, hanging out at the merchandise, or merch, booths or on the street after sets. Emo shows are almost always held at small, intimate clubs and bars, with the rare exception of major acts. Crowd participation in the form of swaying, pogo dancing, moshing, crowd surfing, and singing are still mainstays at emo shows. And most significantly, like British punk rock, American hardcore, and emocore, emo is targeted at teenagers and twentysomethings who feel frustrated, lonely, or alienated.

Emo Idols

One of the most popular emo bands on the scene is Dashboard Confessional.

Emo band Death Cab for Cutie is known for its insightful song lyrics and haunting melodies.

Started in Florida in 2001, the band is centered around lead singer and guitarist Carrabba, who had originally intended it to be a solo project. Dashboard Confessional released several LPs and EPs and has had songs on several blockbuster movie sound tracks, most notably *Spider-Man 2* and *Shrek 2*. The band's music is simple and poppy, mixing acoustic and electric guitars. Carrabba's methods are similar to Jawbreaker's Schwartzenbach's; both write honest and heartfelt lyrics, sometimes straightforward and other times metaphorical. Carrabba has been described as "an open book and he's begging everyone to read it."[36] His good looks, charisma, and genuine lyrics have made him the most revered musician in emo music.

Ben Gibbard of the band Death Cab for Cutie is another admired emo singer. Death Cab was also started as a solo project for Gibbard back in 1997. He is not the prototypical handsome emo heartthrob, but more endearing than his looks are his melancholy voice that is rangy yet common—high but not shrill—and his talent for writing intimate songs. Death Cab guitarist Chris Walla explains:

I feel like the thing Ben does best in his writing is scripting the tiny details and the spaces in between. Like, I would never, ever have thought to write a song ("Title and Registration") that addresses lost love by way of the glove compartment.[37]

The New Jersey Murder Scene

New Jersey has become the home of the most pessimistic emo bands of the early years of the 2000s. Like many other punk rock scenes, living conditions in certain violent and poverty-stricken areas of New Jersey have made a lasting impression on its residents and the bands they created. Gerard Way, vocalist for My Chemical Romance, claims, "Sometimes all we have to do is get up there, make some feedback and say, 'Yeah we're from Noo Jersey,' and then hit 'em like a bomb."[38] His brother Mikey Way, the band's bassist, adds, "I think it gives you a bleak outlook on life. . . . When you're from Jersey, people act like you're from Rikers [a local prison]."[39]

If the perception the Way brothers had about living in New Jersey being like living in a prison, then Geoff Rickly helped lead the prison break. As the

Geoff Rickly, the singer for the band Thursday, performs in 2004. Thursday's distinct sound combines hardcore guitars with emo sentimentality.

singer-songwriter of New Brunswick's Thursday and the cofounder of Eyeball Records, he has become immensely important to the New Jersey scene. As a high school and college student, he would host local hardcore shows in his basement. As he fell more in love with the connection between fans and performers, he tried again to do what he had been unsuccessful at several times before: singing in a band. This time, his bandmates' music inspired him to find his voice. His intellectual and poignant lyrics, combined with the band's immense dedication to its fans, made Thursday an instant crowd favorite. Thursday's first album was the modest *Waiting*, released in 1999 on Eyeball. Its following release was the genre-defining *Full Collapse* on the larger, independent label Victory Records two years later.

On its first two albums, Thursday combines hardcore guitars with emo sentimentality. Their band's sound is far from amateurish; its guitars speed through key and tempo changes, creating different segments in each song, much like progressive rock. What is raw, however, is Rickly's seething voice that is sometimes smooth and sometimes desperately screaming. Most notably, the background vocals also recorded by Rickly are often screamed beyond recording capability and are indeterminable, adding to the intense atmosphere of each song. His lyrics touched on important social issues without being preachy or even political; he considers political bands to

be overbearing and callous. Instead, he writes songs about finding oneself during difficult times and having respect for everyone, using poetic structure, clever wordplay, and educated references to pieces of literature. Thursday never cheats its fans, playing every show like it is the last and staying late afterward to connect with anyone who wants to talk.

Thursday's most striking work was its major-label debut in 2003, *War All the Time*, on Island Def Jam. Songs vary from emocore to quiet piano pieces and deal with the battles people fight every day. These battles range from suicidal thoughts to not becoming a drone. In the album's title track, Rickly sings hauntingly about death on a personal and wide scale, sometimes using imagery associated with the terrorist attack on New York City in 2001. The music video was equally stirring, eerily depicting suburbs as bombing targets. During a benefit show to save CBGB, Rickly explained the song's meaning:

> I always think that our music is very much based in being from here and living here and knowing what it's like to live in this area. This song is about growing up in New Jersey, knowing that there's this big city right across the river from you and it's bigger than anything you could ever imagine. . . . This song is not about 9-11 but this is about what it's like to live in this world now.[40]

Singer Gerard Way of My Chemical Romance seeks inspiration for his songs about vampires and corpses from his favorite comic books.

Rickly's Eyeball Records discovered and signed many other local bands, including Midtown and Murder by Death. His most significant accomplishment was finding My Chemical Romance. Eyeball signed My Chem, and Rickly produced its first album, *I Brought You My Bullets, You Brought Me Your Love*, in 2002. The record was edgy and vast, ranging from the full sound of "Headfirst for Halos" to the sparse and unsettling "Demolition Lovers." Front man Way had previously worked at a comic book store and was inspired by the events of September 11, 2001, to accomplish something more with his life. He drew from his love of comic books to write love songs about vampires and corpses.

Its debut release and energetic live shows earned My Chem a passionate fan base and led to the 2004 release of

Three Cheers for Sweet Revenge on a major label. Heavy touring, with Green Day among others, striking music videos, and hard-rocking, morbid songs made the album a huge success, making My Chem kings of the post-hardcore punk scene. Hit singles included the funeral song "Helena" and the teenage-angst anthem "I'm Not Okay (I Promise)."

Punk Rock Meets Pop Punk

Punk rock finally had come full circle with pop punk, its commercial spin-off, in the middle of 2005. Previously, 1990s pop-punk king Green Day had released its groundbreaking *American Idiot* album in September 2004 to enormous critical acclaim and 8 million in record sales. It was the band's seventh release and a far cry from the immature antics of *Dookie*. Green Day had taken a few stabs at making political statements with singles like "Minority" from its 2000 album, *Warning*. But this time the band had released a full-fledged concept record and a rock opera.

The album starts off with the blistering antiwar song "American Idiot." It was largely an attack on the conservative politics of President George W. Bush and what they perceived as a population of ignorant and paranoid Americans. Green Day also had several other radio hits that were heavily political songs disguised as mainstream pop punk, such as "Holiday" and "Boulevard of Broken Dreams." But the most

artistic and esteemed songs were the two ten-minute epics "Jesus of Suburbia" and "Homecoming."

The entire album, and most notably these two songs, is focused on telling the story of a young man alienated with everything around him. Represented as the Jesus of suburbia, he leaves home and reinvents himself, meeting a rebellious young woman along the way and losing himself even more. The remarkable accomplishment of *American Idiot* is that it tells a story through songs that are great as stand-alones as well.

For the first time ever, a punk rock band received a Grammy nomination for best album of the year in 2005. Green Day did not win that award, but it did beat U2 to win best rock album and record of the year for "Boulevard of Broken Dreams," both unprecedented achievements for punk rock.

In support of the record, the band embarked on a massive worldwide tour starting in 2005. The punk rock movement achieved its greatest popularity and success under Green Day. In front of enormous sold-out arenas and stadiums, drummer Cool and bassist Dirnt jammed while singer and guitarist Armstrong egged on the crowds, reminding them of their civil liberties and personal rights. Wearing neckties from the London punk rock scene and eyeliner from the glam rock scene, the band stood in the spotlight before thousands of admiring fans and in full view of the world. Then, filled with bitterness and irony, in the same way Johnny Rotten had sneered "God Save

Billie Joe Armstrong of Green Day jams during a 2005 show. Green Day is without question the most successful modern-day punk band.

the Queen," Armstrong led the crowd in the reciting of the Pledge of Allegiance.

The Rebellion Continues

Punk rock started as an ironic and rebellious movement that required the major record labels' support in order to initially survive among its mainstream music peers. By the 21st century, however, punk rock had led to the creation of independent record labels, though still helping mainstream labels make millions of dollars. By pushing the music industry's limits into new genres and constantly reinventing its sound, punk rock has secured itself a celebrated past and an enduring future.

• Notes •

Chapter One: Underground Rock

1. Quoted in William McKeen, ed., *Rock and Roll Is Here to Stay*. New York: Norton, 2000, p. 442.
2. Quoted in Tricia Henry, *Break All the Rules*. Ann Arbor: UMI Research Press, 1989, p. 18.
3. Quoted in Stephen Colegrave and Chris Sullivan, *Punk: A Life Apart*. London: Cassell, 2001, p. 30.
4. Quoted in Colegrave and Sullivan, *Punk*, p. 39.
5. Quoted in McKeen, *Rock and Roll Is Here to Stay*, p. 444.
6. Quoted in Nina Antonia, *Iggy Pop*. London: Virgin, 1997.
7. Quote in McKeen, *Rock and Roll Is Here to Stay*, p. 450.
8. Quoted in Jim Miller, ed., *The Rolling Stone Illustrated History of Rock and Roll*. New York: Random House, 1980, p. 553.
9. Quoted in McKeen, *Rock and Roll Is Here to Stay*, p. 451.
10. Quoted in Miller, *The Rolling Stone Illustrated History of Rock and Roll*, p. 553.

Chapter Two: New York, New York

11. *End of the Century: The Story of the Ramones*, DVD, directed by Jim Fields and Michael Gramaglia. New York: Chinagraph, 2003.
12. Legs McNeill, "Escape to New York," *New York Magazine*, April 7, 2003. www.newyorkmetro.com.
13. Quoted in Yvonne Sewell-Ruskin, "Max's Kansas City," The New Colonist. www.newcolonist.com/maxskc.html.
14. Quoted in Paul Taylor, www.maxskansascity.com.
15. *End of the Century*.
16. *End of the Century*.
17. *The Clash: Westway to the World*, DVD, directed by Don Letts. London: 3DD Entertainment, 2000.
18. Hilly Kristal, "The History of CBGB and OMFUG." www.cbgb.com.
19. Quoted in Michael Aron, "Talking Heads: Beyond Safety Pins," *Rolling Stone*, November 17, 1977.
20. Miles, "This Is a Minimalist Headline," *New Musical Express*, April 23, 1977,

Chapter Three: London Calling

21. Henry, *Break All the Rules*, p. xi.
22. Billie Joe Armstrong, "The Sex Pistols," *Rolling Stone*, April 21, 2005, p. 64.
23. Quoted in Miller, *The Rolling Stone Illustrated History of Rock and Roll*, p. 606.
24. *The Clash*.

25. *The Clash*.

Chapter Four: New Wave, Post-Punk, and Hardcore

26. Quoted in Miller, *The Rolling Stone Illustrated History of Rock and Roll*, p. 575.
27. Craig Lee, *Hardcore California*. San Francisco: Last Gasp, 1984, p. 18.
28. Charles O'Hara, *The Philosophy of Punk*. San Francisco: AK, 1999, p. 157.

Chapter Five: Punk Becomes Popular

29. David P. Bianco, *Parents Aren't Supposed to Like It*. New York: UXL, 1998, p. 93.
30. Bianco, *Parents Aren't Supposed to Like It*, p. 97.
31. Andy Greenwald, *Nothing Feels Good*. New York: St. Martin's Griffin, 2003, p. 20.
32. Jim DeRogatis, *Milk It!* Cambridge, MA: Da Capo, 2003, p. 357.
33. Quoted in Anne Hoppus, *blink-182*. New York: Pocket Books, 2001, p. 101.
34. Greenwald, *Nothing Feels Good*, p. 18.

Chapter Six: Punks of the Twenty-first Century

35. Greenwald, *Nothing Feels Good*, p. 19.
36. Greenwald, *Nothing Feels Good*, p. 188.
37. Quoted in Associated Press, "Fame Creeps Up on Death Cab for Cutie," August 30, 2005.
38. Quoted in Dorian Lynskey, "We're Here to Fight Evil," *Blender*, April 2004, p. 94.
39. Quoted in Lynskey, "We're Here to Fight Evil," p. 94.
40. Quoted in CBGB Online. www.cbgb.com/livestreams.htm.

• For More Information •

Books

Mark Andersen, *Dance of Days*. New York: Akashic, 2003. A detailed and close study of the hardcore punk scene in Washington, D.C., that produced bands like Minor Threat, Rites of Spring, and Bad Brains, plus the original straight-edge movement.

Michael Azerrad, *Our Band Could Be Your Life*. Boston: Back Bay, 2002. A book that gives the detailed stories of eleven important independent rock bands between 1981 and 1991, including Minor Threat.

David P. Bianco, *Parents Aren't Supposed to Like It*. New York: UXL, 1998. A series of three volumes that covers 1990s music stars from rock, country, and hip-hop. The book has brief biographies of bands such as Green Day, the Offspring, and Nirvana.

Stephen Colegrave and Chris Sullivan, *Punk: A Life Apart*. London: Cassell, 2001. This book has a large collection of classic punk rock photographs and tells the story of punk completely through testimonials, ranging from its early days to 1990s pop punk.

Luke Crampton and Dafydd Reed, *Rock and Roll Year by Year*. New York: DK, 2003. An extensive, day-by-day account of the first fifty years in rock and roll, starting in 1950 and ending in 2002.

Anthony DeCurtis, James Henke, and Holly George-Warren, eds., *The Rolling Stone Illustrated History of Rock and Roll*. New York: Random House, 1992. An exhaustive collection of stories, testimonials, and contributing writers that covers every important event in the conception and evolution of rock and roll and punk rock.

Jim DeRogatis, *Milk It!* Cambridge, MA: Da Capo, 2003. A collection of articles by an author and music critic for several different magazines and newpapers. The book covers the 1990s alternative music scene, prominently featuring Nirvana.

Andy Greenwald, *Nothing Feels Good*. New York: St. Martin's Griffin, 2003. A contemporary book that covers the whole emo movement from early bands in Washington, D.C., to the most popular bands of the twenty-first century.

Tricia Henry, *Break All the Rules*. Ann Arbor: UMI Research Press, 1989. This book covers the history of punk rock from the Velvet Underground to fanzines, with plenty of quotes and lyrics.

Stuart A. Kallen, *The History of Rock and Roll*. San Diego: Lucent, 2003.

Part of the Music Library series, this is a straightforward recounting of the history of rock and roll, with a portion focused on punk rock.

William McKeen, ed., *Rock and Roll Is Here to Stay*. New York: Norton, 2000. A large collection of biographies and stories of rock-and-roll pioneers, including the Ramones and the Sex Pistols.

Charles O'Hara, *The Philosophy of Punk*. San Francisco: AK, 1999. A great document of the many philosophies and movements of the hardcore punk scene, written by an actual punk rock fan and scene participant.

Movies

The Clash: Westway to the World. DVD. Directed by Don Letts. London: 3DD Entertainment, 2000. A great documentary about the legendary band the Clash, loaded with interesting interviews and tidbits about the band.

End of the Century: The Story of the Ramones. DVD. Directed by Jim Fields and Michael Gramaglia. New York: Chinagraph, 2003. A documentary about the Ramones that features plenty of interviews and classic footage.

Sex Pistols: Never Mind the Bollocks. DVD. Directed by Matthew Longfellow. Los Angeles, CA: Isis Productions, 2002. Another superb documentary that covers the band's ascension and focuses on the making of their historic album, including great special features.

Web Sites

AMG All Music Guide (www.allmusic.com).

Rolling Stone Magazine Online (www.rollingstone.com).

• Index •

• Picture Credits •

• About the Author •

Brenden Masar grew up in San Diego, California, and graduated with a degree in film and media studies from the University of California, Irvine. Presently, he has returned to San Diego, where he has worked on several other projects involving punk rock and other forms of music. He would like to thank Jennifer Skancke for additional help on this book.